Elder Abuse and Neglect in Residential Settings: Different National Backgrounds and Similar Responses

Frank Glendenning, PhD
Paul Kingston, PhD
Editors

The Haworth Maltreatment & Trauma Press
An Imprint of
The Haworth Press, Inc.
New York • London • Oxford

Published by

The Haworth Maltreatment & Trauma Press, 10 Alice Street, Binghamton, NY 13904-1580 USA

The Haworth Maltreatment & Trauma Press is an Imprint of The Haworth Press, Inc., 10 Alice Street, Binghamton, NY 13904-1580 USA.

Elder Abuse and Neglect in Residential Settings: Different National Backgrounds and Similar Responses has also been co-published simultaneously as *Journal of Elder Abuse & Neglect*™, Volume 10, Numbers 1/2 1999.

The Haworth Press, Inc., 10 Alice Street, Binghamton, NY 13904-1580 USA

Cover design by Thomas J. Mayshock Jr.

Library of Congress Cataloging-in-Publication Data

Elder abuse and neglect in residential settings : different national backgrounds and similiar responses / Frank Glendenning, Paul Kingston, guest editors.
    p. cm.
    Published also as v. 10, number 1/2 1999 of Journal of elder abuse & neglect.
    Includes bibliographical references and index.
    ISBN 0-7890-0751-7 (alk. paper)--ISBN 0-7890-0807-6 (pbk. : alk.paper)
    1. Aged–Abuse of. 2. Aged–Institutional care. 3. Nursing home patients–Abuse of. I. Glendenning, Frank. II. Kingston, Paul. III. Journal of elder abuse & neglect.
HV6626.3.E427 1999
362.6–dc21
             99-28084
             CIP

INDEXING & ABSTRACTING

Contributions to this publication are selectively indexed or abstracted in print, electronic, online, or CD-ROM version(s) of the reference tools and information services listed below. This list is current as of the copyright date of this publication. See the end of this section for additional notes.

- *Abstracts in Social Gerontology: Current Literature on Aging*
- *AgeInfo CD-Rom*
- *AgeLine Database*
- *Alzheimer's Disease Education & Referral Center (ADEAR)*
- *Behavioral Medicine Abstracts*
- *Brown University Geriatric Research Application Digest "Abstracts Section"*
- *BUBL Information Service, an Internet-based Information Service for the UK higher education community*
- *Cambridge Scientific Abstracts*
- *caredata CD: the social & community care database*
- *CINAHL (Cumulative Index to Nursing & Allied Health Literature), in print, also on CD-ROM from CD PLUS, EBSCO, and SilverPlatter, and online from CDP Online (formerly BRS), Data-Star, and PaperChase. (Support materials include Subject Heading List, Database Search Guide, and instructional video).*
- *CNPIEC Reference Guide: Chinese National Directory of Foreign Periodicals*
- *Criminal Justice Abstracts*
- *Criminal Justice Periodical Index*
- *Current Contents: Clinical Medicine/Life Sciences (CC:CM/LS) (weekly Table of Contents Service), and Social Science Citation Index. Articles also searchable through Social SciSearch, ISI's online database and in ISI's Research Alert current awareness service.*
- *Educational Administration Abstracts (EAA)*
- *Family Studies Database (online and CD/ROM)*
- *Family Violence & Sexual Assault Bulletin*
- *Human Resources Abstracts (HRA)*
- *IBZ International Bibliography of Periodical Literature*
- *Index to Periodical Articles Related to Law*

(continued)

- *MasterFILE: updated database from EBSCO Publishing*
- *Mental Health Abstracts (online through DIALOG)*
- *National Criminal Justice Reference Service*
- *New Literature on Old Age*
- *Sage Family Studies Abstracts (SFSA)*
- *Sage Urban Studies Abstracts (SUSA)*
- *Social Planning/Policy & Development Abstracts (SOPODA)*
- *Social Work Abstracts*
- *Sociological Abstracts (SA)*
- *Violence and Abuse Abstracts: A Review of Current Literature on Interpersonal Violence (VAA)*

Special Bibliographic Notes related to special journal issues (separates) and indexing/abstracting:

- indexing/abstracting services in this list will also cover material in any "separate" that is co-published simultaneously with Haworth's special thematic journal issue or DocuSerial. Indexing/abstracting usually covers material at the article/chapter level.
- monographic co-editions are intended for either non-subscribers or libraries which intend to purchase a second copy for their circulating collections.
- monographic co-editions are reported to all jobbers/wholesalers/approval plans. The source journal is listed as the "series" to assist the prevention of duplicate purchasing in the same manner utilized for books-in-series.
- to facilitate user/access services all indexing/abstracting services are encouraged to utilize the co-indexing entry note indicated at the bottom of the first page of each article/chapter/contribution.
- this is intended to assist a library user of any reference tool (whether print, electronic, online, or CD-ROM) to locate the monographic version if the library has purchased this version but not a subscription to the source journal.
- individual articles/chapters in any Haworth publication are also available through the Haworth Document Delivery Service (HDDS).

Elder Abuse and Neglect in Residential Settings: Different National Backgrounds and Similar Responses

CONTENTS

Preface

We are extremely grateful to our colleagues around the world who agreed almost immediately to contribute to this special publication of *Journal of Elder Abuse & Neglect.* We are indebted to Roger Clough, Gabrielle Griffin, Lynda Aitken, Britt-Inger Saveman, Sture Åström, Gösta Bucht, Astrid Norberg, Ruth Chambers, Susan J. Aziz, Irene Campbell-Taylor, Alison Brammer, Ariela Lowenstein, Gerna Conradie, and Mike Nolan.

The volume of elder abuse and neglect in residential settings, we believe, is timely. It is clearly necessary to extend the knowledge base on elder abuse and neglect found in institutions to colleagues in other countries. This is especially important for countries where developments have been perhaps slower than in those represented in this monograph. Insights gained from countries where elder abuse and neglect have been recognised as an issue requiring social policy attention can motivate individuals in other countries who may believe that they are a lone voice to which politicians and professionals would rather not listen. We hope that this collection helps to contribute to greater understanding about elder abuse and neglect worldwide.

Paul Kingston, PhD
Frank Glendenning, PhD

Elder Abuse and Neglect
in Residential Settings:
The Need for Inclusiveness
in Elder Abuse Research

Frank Glendenning, PhD

SUMMARY. This introductory paper argues that research into elder abuse and neglect has become locked in the family violence model, whereas in reality much more research attention needs to be paid to abuse in residential settings as well. Relevant research findings during the last fifteen years are reviewed. Special attention is paid to the work of Pillemer in America and Clough in England. During the course of the paper the remaining articles in this volume will also be reviewed, with attention being drawn to the importance of several aspects of nursing care in this context: quality, restraint, nutrition, and over-medication. *[Article copies available for a fee from The Haworth Document Delivery Service: 1-800-342-9678. E-mail address: getinfo@haworthpressinc.com]*

KEYWORDS. Older people, residential centres, hospitals, nursing homes, care homes

The dominant approach to elder mistreatment in the research literature has been to apply the family violence model. This has tended to

Frank Glendenning is Honorary Senior Research Fellow, Centre for Social Gerontology, Keele University, Staffordshire, UK.

Address correspondence to: Frank Glendenning, 32 Dartmouth Avenue, Newcastle-under-Lyme, Staffordshire, ST5 3NY, UK.

[Haworth co-indexing entry note]: "Elder Abuse and Neglect in Residential Settings: The Need for Inclusiveness in Elder Abuse Research." Glendenning, Frank. Co-published simultaneously in *Journal of Elder Abuse & Neglect* (The Haworth Maltreatment & Trauma Press, an imprint of The Haworth Press, Inc.) Vol. 10, No. 1/2, 1999, pp. 1-11; and: *Elder Abuse and Neglect in Residential Settings: Different National Backgrounds and Similar Responses* (ed: Frank Glendenning, and Paul Kingston) The Haworth Press, Inc., 1999, pp. 1-11. Single or multiple copies of this article are available for a fee from The Haworth Document Delivery Service [1-800-342-9678, 9:00 a.m. - 5:00 p.m. (EST). E-mail address: getinfo@haworthpressinc.com].

underplay our concern about the manifestations of mistreatment in residential settings (hospitals, nursing homes, and residential care homes). So, while the extent of abuse in informal and family settings is still very unclear, its existence within British institutions at least has been widely documented (Glendenning, 1993, 1997; Phillipson & Biggs, 1985; see also Clough, this volume), even though there are no prevalence studies.

When discussing this subject, it has been customary to draw a distinction between individual acts of abuse in institutions and actual institutional or institutionalized abuse. As Decalmer (1993, 59) has suggested, abuse of the person is common, but 'the commonest abuse of all is institutional abuse, where the environment, practices, and rules become abusive in themselves' (see also Hughes, 1996; Aitken & Griffin, 1996; Peace, Kellaher & Willcocks, 1997; Glendenning, 1996, 1997). Bennett and Kingston have argued that there is a deficiency in research that could be used to explain and remedy the socialization processes that lead to abusing behaviour in institutions (Bennett & Kingston, 1993, 116) and indeed there are no longitudinal studies that would enable us to examine the influence of age, or indeed other variables, like health status, and availability of family care, on the probability of moving into residential care.

Awareness of elder abuse in the home may be traced in Britain to correspondence in the medical press during the 1970s (Baker, 1975; Burston, 1975, 1977). By that time Townsend had already published his dramatic study of institutions in *The Last Refuge* (1962). Kingston has recently drawn attention to a letter in *The Times* of London in 1965, signed by a group of the 'great and the good' drawing attention to the shocking treatment of some elderly patients in certain mental hospitals (Kingston, 1997: 78) thus indicating that mistreatment and neglect in long-stay institutions was recognized in Britain in the early 1960s.

It is, however, possible to trace historically the findings of American investigators since the early 1970s. As long ago as 1973, Stannard published a paper in *Social Problems* entitled 'Old folks and dirty work' based on his participant observation study of a nursing home in which he identified slapping, hitting, shaking, hair pulling, tightening restraining belts, and terrorizing by gesture or word (Stannard, 1973). In the same year, coincidentally, the fine novelist, May Sarton, published a novel (*As We Are Now*) which took as its theme, the mistreatment of elderly residents in a nursing home based on an actual experience when visiting a friend of hers in New Hampshire, as reported in an interview, twenty years later (Ingersoll, 1991: 203).

In 1981, Kimsey, Tarbox, and Bragg examined 1,000 nursing homes in Texas and reported that deliberate physical abuse was known but less common than physical neglect: that is, patients with bedsores, poor nutrition, improper medication, and vermin infestation. They compiled a profile of the total nursing home population in Texas of 70,000 people and found that the average age was 82 years, 95 per cent were over 65, and 70 per cent over 79. The ratio of women to men was 2:1; most patients were poor and isolated; more than 50 per cent had some mental impairment; half had no close relatives; and fewer than 50 per cent could walk alone (Kimsey et al., 1981).

Tarbox followed this report with a paper on the psychological aspects of neglect in nursing homes, emphasizing uncleanliness, lack of attractiveness in the physical environment, inadequate diet, infantilization, and passive neglect (Tarbox, 1983). In the same year, Doty and Sullivan reported their findings of a study of the statistics of the federal certification agency based on a sample of 550 skilled nursing facilities nation-wide with 54,000 beds and as of September, 1980, 7 per cent were cited by the agency as being deficient in relation to patients' rights, policies, and procedures. In their study of New York City Nursing Homes, there was evidence of patients who were unable to feed themselves and were not being fed. They noted that patient abuse, neglect, and mistreatment were often dismissed on the grounds that the evidence was anecdotal (Doty & Sullivan, 1983: 223).

In 1980, 3,000 cases of potential Medicaid fraud in different states were investigated. In reviewing the findings, Halamandaris listed a cavalcade of abuse in nursing homes: theft from patients' funds, false claims by carers to Medicare and Medicaid, trading in real estate, fraudulent therapy and pharmaceutical charges, and even involvement in organised crime (Halamandaris, 1983, 104-14). Stathopoulos also reported on the development of consumer advocacy strategies in nursing homes in north central Massachusetts and reflected that 'elder abuse in institutions is one part of the continuum of abuse in our society. Public policy which supports institutionalization of the elderly to the exclusion of other forms of care in the community is in many instances the root of elder abuse in institutions' (Stathopoulos, 1983, 353).

Then Solomon investigated the pharmacological and non-pharmacological abuse of elderly patients by health care professionals and concluded that 'poorly trained caretakers can command lesser pay but have an extremely high turnover rate . . . The frustrations of the job and the debility of the patients promote infantilization, derogation, and actual physical abuse' (Solomon, 1983, 159). Later, Cowell described the progress made in California in the 1980s which instituted a statewide study of the quality of care in nursing homes (Blum, 1987). This led to legislation to deal with alleged abuse and neglect in health care facilities that received state medical insurance payments. Cowell suggested, however, that legislation on its own would not bring about change (Cowell, 1989).

Finally in 1990, Fader et al. published a paper on a study of health care workers in long-term care settings in New York and the way in which they perceived elder abuse in relation to active and passive neglect. Nurse aides were found to have significantly lower scores than licensed practical nurses and other groups. The researchers concluded that ongoing education and training was essential.

Apart from the Texas study, however, there was not another thorough review of abuse in nursing homes until that by Pillemer and Moore in 1987 (Pillemer & Moore, 1989, 1990), which Pillemer revisited with Lachs in 1995 (Lachs & Pillemer, 1995). Bennett and Kingston, reflecting in 1993 on their work from a British perspective suggested that Pillemer and Moore's findings set alongside the British official enquiry reports led them to the conclusion that abuse in institutions is relatively widespread.

Pillemer and Moore believed that any statistics about known cases of maltreatment were likely to be underestimates of the actual incidence. They invoked the 1984 study by Monk et al. that found that over half the nursing home residents in their sample were fearful of reprisals if they complained–a point that had not escaped Sarton in her 1970s novel. This was well documented by Pillemer and Moore in their random survey of nursing home staff in one state. Because of its pivotal importance, the study has been cited by others, especially in Britain so that it might reach a wider public (Bennett & Kingston, 1993, 125-6; Keller, 1996: 221; Glendenning, 1996, 42-3; 1997, 155-6).

The data obtained through the survey demonstrated that staff were motivated by a desire to help others and to have meaningful employment, but 32 per cent felt the job to be very stressful. Lack of time was given as one reason for stress and the more personalized tasks like walking, talking, and helping residents with personal care activities were identified as the ones not done (see also Baillon et al., 1996: 223).

When all the data were collected, thirty-two per cent were classified by Pillemer and Moore as being in the 'high burnout category.' They went on to show that burnout was strongly related to stress and therefore reducing stress should be a high priority for administrators. Training in the management of patient behaviour and aggression was also seen to be critical.

Thirty-six per cent of the sample had seen at least one act of physical abuse during the preceding year. Seventy per cent had seen staff insult or swear at patients during the preceding year. Forty per cent had committed at least one act of psychological abuse during the preceding year. The authors suggested that as the survey was based on self-reporting, some under-reporting probably occurred and although these estimates cannot be compared with compatible data, there is 'sufficiently extensive evidence to merit concern' (Pillemer & Moore, 1989: 314-20). Pillemer extended this investigation with Brachman-Prehn to determine the predictors of negative actions. They concluded that well-qualified staff do not choose to work in nursing homes. Pillemer had already reported that the work is physically taxing, wages are poor, and job prestige is low (Pillemer, 1988: 232). He also drew attention to the quality of care in nursing homes which employed trained nurses and where the staff-patient ratios were relatively high. As a result of these studies, Pillemer developed with Hudson and others a model programme for nursing assistants called 'Ensuring an Abuse-Free Environment' (CARIE, 1991). This was later described in a paper (Pillemer & Hudson, 1993) and also by Hudson Keller (1996).

Another element for staff working in situations of very high conflict is the risk of verbal and physical assault by patients. This is not confined to American nursing homes. Similar findings were reported in a recent study in Bristol, England (Eastley et al., 1993) and also in a study in Manitoba, Canada. The latter demonstrated that in a 320-bed long-term care facility, 1134 incidents of physical aggression occurred each month, which meant that a typical nursing assistant could expect to be physically assaulted 9.3 times a month. The majority of nursing assistants were insulted or sworn at, experiencing this behavior as an ongoing fact of life, with 1365 incidents of aggression being reported; that is, 11.3 on a monthly basis (Goodridge, Johnston, & Thomson, 1996, 49-65). Burnout, they conclude, is 'probably far more prevalent than previously realized' (p. 63).

So far we have only discussed American and Canadian evidence, but clearly this can be repeated from the experience of other countries, as the papers in this volume demonstrate. I have suggested elsewhere that what is remarkable is that Pillemer in the USA and Clough in England, working independently at the same time in the 1980s and with different research models, arrived at similar conclusions (Glendenning 1997: 160), namely that there is a model of patient maltreatment which relates to three key factors: (1) the environment of the nursing home, (2) the characteristics of the staff and (3) the characteristics of the patients, together with external factors that may need to be taken into account (Pillemer, 1988; Clough, 1988; see also Biggs, Phillipson, & Kingston, 1995; Glendenning, 1996, 1997).

In one of the papers that follow, Clough breaks the silence that in reality was imposed upon him unwillingly at the time of the Wagner Committee on Residential Care in 1988. He discusses two of the inquiry reports that he reviewed in his unpublished report *Scandals in Residential Centres*. Clough had published *Old Age Homes* in 1981, but at that time the discourse about elder mistreatment had not really begun in Britain. In preparing his 1988 report, what he found appalled him, as he movingly describes. That his findings have never seen the light of day until very recently, can only be because they were unpalatable to the Establishment at the time and his report, although prepared at the Committee's request, was never embodied in its own final document (Glendenning, 1996: 47).

What becomes clear from the American and Canadian research, together with the work of Clough and others in Britain is that until Pillemer and Hudson's work in 1991 there was never a model available for training in this type of work. Only recently has it been receiving attention in Britain (Clough, 1994, 1996 a, b and c; Pritchard, 1996). We have not included a paper specifically on education and training, although its importance is mentioned several times in the papers that follow.

Additionally, investigators agree that another central problem confronting nursing in long-term care (LTC) is burnout and how to deal with it. Griffin and Aitken in their timely paper in this volume about gender issues also insist that inspection units are overstretched and that, complain as we may about the lack of government commitment in Britain to research in residential institutions (Glendenning, 1996: 48), the government has little incentive to do so as it relies on residential settings to implement its fund-starved policies. In fact, the whole issue of LTC has already reached international proportions, with its implications for the investment of resources. It is clear that we are soon approaching the time when one in four of the population in some industrialized countries will be over 80 and one in four of the over-85s will suffer from dementia (Binstock et al., 1992).

There is already sufficient research information to demonstrate that the study of elder abuse and neglect needs to embrace not only the family violence model, but the clear implication that in institutional settings there is a paramount need for better training, better working conditions, and a fundamental recognition by administrators and managers that burnout is an established phenomenon; and we ignore it at our, and more particularly, the patient's peril.

Saveman's early empirical studies of elder mistreatment in different parts of Sweden during the early 1990s were based on interviews with families, district nurses, and home care assistants. While she did not believe that findings from the USA in particular could necessarily illuminate the situation in her own country at that stage (Saveman, 1994, 17), she noted that with the absence of policy guidelines in Sweden, each profession appeared to respond to situations of abuse on its own terms, commenting 'public policy should be clarified' (p. 185). She concluded that there needed to be a much more serious study of this social problem in domestic settings, and her findings were remarkably similar to those of others in the English-speaking countries. She has moved more recently into an examination of abuse and neglect in residential care homes and the findings of her research team are included below. They emphasise that there is clear evidence of mistreatment in care homes for old people in Sweden, resulting in the fearfulness, aggression, and withdrawal of the abused persons. The staff felt powerless and inadequate and further research and improved education and training of staff who are experiencing exhaustion and burnout is clearly indicated.

The paper authored by Nolan deals with the important issue of quality of nursing care in residential care and nursing homes. Like Griffin and Aitken, he emphasises the need for a greater investment of resources, returning to the Williams Report (1967) which maintained that there was no hope of any significant improvement in the number and quality of staff unless there could be a significant injection of finance. Given the current state of public expenditure in Britain and the sensitive matter of private sector finance, there is every indication that because the implications are so far-reaching, the LTC of the old will remain a 'Cinderella service' with all that that implies for both residents and staff. Yet Nolan reiterates the undeniable fact that there is a need for what he terms 'creating a quality perception.'

Also included in this issue is a paper by Chambers on the potential for the abuse of medication in care homes. It reminds me vividly of the 1983 papers by Halamandaris and Solomon mentioned above and serves as yet another reminder of the existence of unscrupulous health professionals and sloppy professional practice, suggesting a number of measures that may be taken to control or at least minimise such abuse.

In addition to the abuse of medication, we include also a paper by Aziz and Campbell-Taylor on under-nutrition and malnutrition in long term care. These are merely two of a series of issues that are coming to the fore as a deeper awareness of abuse in institutions and residential settings occurs. Restraint (see Parker & Miles, 1997) has already emerged as an issue that requires further study, together with, as far as the UK is concerned, urgent and continual attention to the system of the regulation of residential care. Brammer, for example, addresses in her paper the legal powers of the Registered Home Tribunal and the Registration Authority in the UK and does a careful analysis of what constitutes a 'fit person.'

Lowenstein, in her review of abuse in residential settings in contemporary Israel, adds further evidence of the existence of such mistreatment, exercised in the main by nurses' aides. Her findings confirm much of what we already know. Conradie, writing from a South African perspective, shows that legislation does not necessarily protect elderly people against abusive treatment (cf. Cowell, 1989) and notes the enormous disparity between penalties for elder and child abuse. Common law neglect is not a punishable offence in South Africa. She analyses abuse in institutions in relation to social policy, legislation and cultural diversity and care delivery systems, noting the lack of understanding of cultural practices and traditions which exists between previously segregated groups as a result of the apartheid system in South Africa. Her paper underlines the necessity for controlled research in South Africa. She argues that both management and carers must be willing to move through training and education from a primarily unicultural standpoint to one of respect and appreciation for cultural diversity and refers to the complication of the likelihood of finding several indigenous languages being used in one particular residential setting. This is beginning to become potentially a visible issue in Britain, adding weight to the growing demand by British Health Service researchers for an increased provision of trained bi-lingual support workers who can act with multi-cultural awareness, both as interpreters (with multi-language ability, especially in South Asian languages), health promoters, and advocates (Duncan, 1989; Leather & Wirz, 1996).

What emerges from all the recently written papers in this volume is that there are many elements which are deeply significant for residential care that need to be employed in future studies of elder abuse and neglect. These elements include a deeper understanding of the nursing task itself, the nature of these institutions and their environment, the characteristics of patients and staff, the importance of developing gender-integrated and multi-cultural theories of elder abuse in residential as well as in domestic settings, and the urgent need for prevalence studies of abuse in residential settings. We cannot rely simply on the family violence model.

REFERENCES

Aitken, L. & Griffin, G. (1996). *Gender issues in elder abuse.* London: Sage Publications.

Baillon, S., Boyle, A., Neville, P.G. & Scothern, G. (1996). Factors that contribute to stress in care staff in nursing homes for the elderly, *International Journal of Geriatric Psychiatry,* 11: 219-26.

Baker, A.A. (1975). Granny battering, *Modern Geriatrics,* 5(8): 20-4.

Bennett, G.C.J. & Kingston, P. (1993). *Elder abuse: Concepts, theories and interventions.* London: Chapman and Hall.

Binstock, R.H., Post, S.G. & Whitehouse, P.J. (1992). The challenges of dementia. In *Dementia and aging: Ethics, values and policy choices.* Baltimore: Johns Hopkins University Press, pp. 1-17.

Burston, G.R. (1975). Granny battering, *British Medical Journal,* 6 September: 92.

Burston, G.R. (1977). Do your elderly patients live in fear of being battered? *Modern Geriatrics,* 7(5): 54-5.

Clough, R. (1981). *Old age homes.* London: Allen and Unwin.

Clough, R. (1988). *Scandals in residential centres.* A report to the Wagner Committee (unpublished).

Clough, R. (ed.) (1996). *The abuse of care in residential institutions* CARIE (Coalition for the Rights of the Infirm Elderly) *Ensuring an Abuse-Free Environment: A Learning Program for Nursing Home Staff.* Philadelphia: CARIE.

Cowell, A. (1989). Abuse of the institutionalized aged: Recent policy in California. In R. Filinson & S.R. Ingham (eds.) *Elder abuse practice and policy.* New York: Human Sciences Press, pp. 242-54.

Doty, P. & Sullivan, E.W. (1983). Community involvement in combatting abuse, neglect and mistreatment in nursing homes. *Milbank Fund Quarterly/Health and Society,* 32: 222-51.

Duncan, D. (ed.) (1989). *Working with bi-lingual disability.* London: Chapman Hall.

Decalmer, P. (1993). Clinical presentation. In P. Decalmer & F. Glendenning (eds). *The mistreatment of elderly people* (First edition). London: Sage Publications, pp. 35-61.

Eastley, R.J., Macpherson, R., Richards, H. & Mia, T.H. (1993). Assaults on professional carers of elderly people. *British Medical Journal,* 307: 845.

Fader, A., Koge, N., Gupta, G.L. & Gambert, S.R. (1990). Perceptions of elder abuse by health care workers in a long-term care setting. *Clinical Gerontologist,* 10(2): 292-8.

Glendenning, F. (1996). The mistreatment of elderly people in residential institutions. In R. Clough (ed.), *op.cit.* pp. 35-49.

Glendenning, F. (1997). The mistreatment and neglect of elderly people in residential centres: Research outcomes. In P. Decalmer & F. Glendenning (eds.), *op.cit.* (2nd edition), pp. 151-62.

Goodridge, D.M., Johnston, P. & Thomson, M. (1996). Conflict and aggression as stressors in the work environment of nursing assistants: Implications for institutional elder abuse. *Journal of Elder Abuse & Neglect,* 8 (1): 49-67.

Halamandaris, V.J. (1983). Fraud and abuse in nursing homes. In J.I. Kosberg (ed.), *op.cit.*

Hughes, B. (1995). *Older people and community care: Critical theory and practice.* Buckingham: Open University Press.

Ingersoll, E.G. (ed.) (1991). *Conversations with May Sarton.* Jackson, MS: University of Mississippi Press.

Keller, B.H. (1996). A model abuse prevention training program for long-term care staff. In L.A. Baumhover & S.C. Beall (eds.), *Abuse, neglect and exploitation of older persons.* London: Jessica Kingsley Publishers, pp. 221-40.

Kimsey, L.R., Tarbox, A.R. & Bragg, D.F. (1981). Abuse of the elderly: The hidden agenda. 1. The caretaker and the categories of abuse. *American Geriatrics Society Journal,* 29: 465-72.

Kingston, P. (1997). Institutional dimensions. In Bennett, G.C.J., Kingston, P. & Penhale, B. *The dimensions of elder abuse.* London: Macmillan, pp. 70-99.

Kosberg, J.I. (1983). *Abuse and maltreatment of the elderly: Causes and interventions.* Boston: John Wright.

Lachs, M.S. & Pillemer, K.A. (1995). Abuse and neglect of elderly persons. *New England Journal of Medicine*, 33297: 437-43.

Leather, C. & Wirz, S. (1996). *The training and development needs of bi-lingual support workers in the NHS in community settings.* London: University of London.

Maslach, C. (1982). *Burnout: The cost of caring.* Englewood Cliffs, N.J.: Prentice-Hall.

Monk, A., Kaye, L.W. & Litwin, M. (1984). *Resolving grievances in the nursing home: A study of the ombudsman's program.* New York: Columbia University Press.

Peace, S., Kellaher, L. & Willcocks, D. (1997). *Re-evaluating residential care.* Buckingham: Open University Press.

Parker, K. & Miles, S.H. (1997). Deaths caused by bedrails. *Journal of the American Geriatrics Society*, 45(7): 797-802.

Pillemer, K.A. (1988). Maltreatment of patients in nursing homes. *Journal of Health and Social Behaviour*, 29(3): 227-38.

Pillemer, K.A. & Brachman-Prehn, R. (1991). Helping and hurting: Predictors of maltreatment of patients in nursing homes. *Research on Aging*, 13(1): 74-95.

Pillemer, K.A. (1989). Abuse of patients in nursing homes: Findings from a survey of staff. *The Gerontologist*, 29(3): 51-7.

Pillemer, K.A. & Moore, D.W. (1990). Highlights from a study of abuse in nursing homes. *Journal of Elder Abuse & Neglect*, 2 (1/2): 5-29.

Pritchard, J. (1996). *Working with elder abuse: A training manual for home care, residential and day care staff.* London: Jessica Kingsley Publishers.

Saveman, B.I. (1994). *Formal carers in healthcare and the social services witnessing the abuse of the elderly in their homes.* Umea, Sweden: Umea University.

Sarton, M. (1983). *As we are now.* London: The Women's Press.

Solomon, K. (1983). Intervention for victimized elderly and sensitization of health professionals. In J.I. Kosberg (ed.), *op.cit.*

Stannard, C. (1973). Old folks and dirty work: The social conditions for patient abuse in a nursing home. *Social Problems*, 20: 329-42.

Stathopoulos, P.A. (1983). Consumer advocacy and abuse of elders in nursing homes. In J.I. Kosberg (ed.), *op.cit.*

Tarbox, A.R. (1983). The elderly in nursing homes: Psychological aspects of neglect. *Clinical Gerontologist*, 1: 39-52.

Townsend, P. (1962). *The last refuge.* London: Routledge & Kegan Paul.

Wagner Committee (1988). *Residential care: A positive choice.* Report of the Independent Review of Residential Care. Vol. 1. London: HMSO.

Williams Report (1967). *Caring for people: Staffing residential homes.* London: National Council of Social Service.

Scandalous Care:
Interpreting Public Enquiry Reports of Scandals in Residential Care

Roger Clough, MA

SUMMARY. This article reviews an earlier study written for the Wagner Committee (1988) on scandals in residential care. That review was based on a study of ten enquiry reports, only two of which were about homes for older people. The main events that were described are grouped as: institutionalised practices, indifference and neglect, physical cruelty, humiliation, too authoritarian a life-style, a dull and depressing life-style, an overcrowded and run down environment, disharmony amongst the staff team, and staff misappropriating goods or money. Now, more weight should be given to: residents' abuse of residents and of staff, an improper influence on the life-style of others, and sexual abuse. Explanations proposed are: structural, environmental, and individual and worker style. Abuse is considered in the context of the nature of direct care and the acts of intimate caring of others. *[Article copies available for a fee from The Haworth Document Delivery Service: 1-800-342-9678. E-mail address: getinfo@haworthpressinc.com]*

KEYWORDS. Abuse, neglect, staff disharmony, physical cruelty, work style

INTRODUCTION

The experience of reading numbers of reports about scandalous care is profound. 'Instead of being hardened, I have become punch

---

Roger Clough is Professor of Social Work, Lancaster University, UK, Department of Applied Social Science, Cartmel College, The University, Lancaster, LA1 4YL, UK.

[Haworth co-indexing entry note]: "Scandalous Care: Interpreting Public Enquiry Reports of Scandals in Residential Care." Clough, Roger. Co-published simultaneously in *Journal of Elder Abuse & Neglect* (The Haworth Maltreatment & Trauma Press, an imprint of The Haworth Press, Inc.) Vol. 10, No. 1/2, 1999, pp. 13-27; and: *Elder Abuse and Neglect in Residential Settings: Different National Backgrounds and Similar Responses* (ed: Frank Glendenning, and Paul Kingston) The Haworth Press, Inc., 1999, pp. 13-27. Single or multiple copies of this article are available for a fee from The Haworth Document Delivery Service [1-800-342-9678, 9:00 a.m. - 5:00 p.m. (EST). E-mail address: getinfo@haworthpressinc.com].

drunk: angry, helpless, dejected and with a feeling of revolt in my stomach' (Clough, 1988). These were words I wrote as part of an unpublished review of reports on scandals for the Wagner Committee. In this article I aim to review that earlier study. I draw on three and a half years heading Cumbria's registration and inspection service (Clough, 1994) and my more recent study of abuse in residential homes (Clough, 1996a, b and c).

The review for the Wagner Committee was based on a study of ten enquiry reports into: six individual child care establishments, all the residential homes for older people of a London borough, a home for older people, a secure hospital, and a hospital for people with learning disabilities (in today's terminology). In addition I examined a research study of four different hospitals for children with disabilities; significantly these were the only establishments that had not been selected for examination because someone had judged that there were serious problems within the establishments. The reports covered thirty years with the most recent having been written in 1987.

Thus it is essential to note at the outset the limited and partial nature of the evidence: it comprised reports I had on hand and was not selected to be representative. In that earlier study and in this article I have not attempted to provide an overview of all reports into scandals. A further important fact is that only two of the reports focus on older people, though both were the most recent of those I studied. For this paper I draw primarily on these two reports, testing points against the wider sample.

The Context

Drawing attention to bad residential practice is problematic for those currently working with integrity in residential care because it has the potential to undermine further work, which for other reasons holds low status and is undervalued. Of course, there is nothing to be gained by sweeping the dirt under the carpet. Yet the problem remains. Because we know little about the scale of abuse, we cannot position the scandalous events in the totality of residential care for older people. We do not know what proportion of care is (i) good, (ii) good enough, (iii) below standard, and (iv) appalling. Further, there are dilemmas in drawing attention to particular places when reports on other homes have not been examined and when we would have to recognise that some, perhaps most, of the known appalling practices have not been reported in this way. Yet such identification is a necessary part of quoting from the source material.

In the next section I set out the main events described under a number of headings which are my grouping of the events. The act of description raises various points: 'Where does bad practice end and abuse begin?' 'To what extent were events typical of the whole life within that home or other homes?'; that is, questions as to pervasiveness.

The Events Reported

The accounts which follow are drawn from the reports. They are the interpretations of those appointed to investigate. Further questions follow: who selects? on what basis? how do they collect their evidence? under what terms of reference and authority do they operate? I cover some of these points from my experience in conducting enquiries (Clough, 1996) and the report on Camden's residential homes for older people (Camden, 1987).

> Following a complaint, the London Borough of Camden asked me to hold an independent review of its residential homes for older people. I reported that there was a poor standard of care in most homes, with institutionalised practice, residents having little choice or ability to take initiative. Buildings were poor; in older homes too many shared rooms; purpose built homes were too large and impersonal. Older people from ethnic minorities were likely to find the experience particularly daunting. Overall the care of older people was given a low priority in the social services department (SSD) and 'effective management of residential care in Camden had broken down.' 'Again and again we were informed of a sense of helplessness about being able to manage the residential services in Camden.' (Camden, 1987, p. 4)

The second report on which I drew was that into Nye Bevan Lodge in Southwark (Gibbs, Evans, & Rodway, 1987). Of all the reports, this one, along with one on Ely Hospital, provides the most dramatic example of a single establishment where bad practice and cruelty were pervasive.

> The atmosphere of deep distrust and suspicion which permeated every aspect of life in the Home for many years resulting in a serious deterioration in the level of care provided, was such that a

proper level of caring could never be restored given the same staff and officers. We have come to the conclusion that over a period of years certain care assistants behaved in an uncaring and insensitive manner to the residents, often in circumstances which amounted to ill treatment and cruelty. (Gibbs, Evans, & Rodway 1987, p. 136)

The catalogue of events is alarming. Listing the factors does not mean that these events happened to each older person each day. But they were frequent episodes, were more likely to happen to particular residents, and were perpetrated by a small number of staff. The events included:

- Neglecting to care, in particular to wash or bathe; charging residents for bathing, perhaps, to restrict numbers as well as to make extra money;
- Punishing residents who complained or were thought to be a nuisance: Leaving one person's feet in a bowl of excessively hot water, opening windows and removing blankets at night; some residents caught pneumonia and died;
- Some residents had falls after altercations with staff;
- Use of the bar in the home by a few staff and outsiders who were rowdy and sometimes molested staff or residents;
- Institutionalised practices, such as lining up three naked women in order to bathe them.

In my paper I grouped the findings of the reports into categories and reported under these, with some comment as to their appropriateness.

Institutionalised Practices Whereby Residents Were Treated en Masse. In the Camden report this finding holds perhaps the overwhelming weight

Residents were awakened up too early (5.45-6.30 a.m.); had little choice or flexibility as to going to bed: had little opportunity for getting snacks or drinks for themselves and little choice at meals; were served the last meal too early at 5.30 p.m. or before; had few personal possessions; there was a lack of proper procedures and personnel for washing, mending and marking clothes; 'clothing . . . is often dirty and unkempt, often with no underwear and in particular there is an absence of knickers.'

The example of people being lined up for baths, already quoted from Nye Bevan fits into this section.

Indifference and Neglect. Much of what happened at Nye Bevan can be summarised under this heading. It relates to the staff's interpretation of their work and to attitudes towards the older people who were residents.

> The most important objective for care assistants seems to have been finding time for socialising with each other, either in the staff room or in the lounge; but always at a distance from the residents. When looking at television, especially the afternoon soap operas, the residents were considered an inconvenience to be put out of the way as quickly as possible. (Gibbs, Evans, & Rodway, p. 76)

A recurring theme in the reports is that of leaving people in urine soaked clothes. In the Camden report one man

> was reported as having been found by a visiting doctor so soaked in urine that it made a 'high tide' mark, which would have taken up to seven hours to form across his shirt and was so depressed that he had ceased to be able to maintain any form of self care. After a few days in hospital, he had fully recovered. (Camden, p. 63)

Physical Cruelty. These categories merge into one another. Assaults have often been the trigger for investigations, perhaps because they are easier to identify or to take action about than neglect. This is not a feature of the Camden report. It is commonly reported about the children's establishments in this study and in part may relate to the extent to which staff find control of residents problematic. At Nye Bevan some residents were threatened with a slap if they did not do what they were told. Categorising some other acts is difficult because they contain elements of neglect and assault. One care assistant on at least one occasion put faeces into the mouth of a resident. As I have mentioned, residents were at times punished by having windows left open and covers stripped from their beds.

Humiliation. At Nye Bevan, staff wheeled an incontinent resident round the home to show her to the officers. One officer said: 'It was as if the residents weren't people–they would laugh at them . . . just a pet that you weren't inclined to be kind to . . . ' (Gibbs, Evans, & Rodway, p. 72). The power of staff in the day to day lives of residents is apparent and because of this the direct care staff have the most impact on residents' lives.

Too Authoritarian a Life Style. In my earlier report I had noted nothing under this heading relating to the homes for older people, although some of the activities such as lining up people to wait for baths could be categorised in this section rather than under that of institutionalised practices.

A Dull and Depressing Life Style. At Camden:

> The great majority of residents are no longer able to initiate activities for themselves without encouragement. . . . apart from an occasional session of music and movement, bingo and community singing . . . residents spend most of their time watching television or doing nothing at all. We were particularly concerned to find a notice board with details of activities that were to take place and in fact never did. (Camden, p. 25)

Overcrowded and Run Down Environments. The most appalling examples of inadequate buildings were in the reports on large hospitals. In Camden's residential facilities there were some aspects that were poor and certainly had failed to keep pace with general building improvements. For example, in one older home a downstairs lavatory was inaccessible to people in wheel chairs or with walking frames. Other examples were the dining room which could not accommodate the number of residents and bathrooms off residents' rooms so the rooms of residents became used as corridors for other residents en route to their baths.

Disharmony Among Staff Team. The range of potential conflicts is apparent in the following quotation from the Camden report:

> Some staff members expressed themselves as deeply distressed at their inability to offer good care, because some colleagues did not carry out their duties responsibly, refused orders, and [were] aggressive and abusive. . . . We heard allegations of fights amongst staff members and of staff having to be escorted to public transport because of fear of retribution from other staff members. We heard of great unrest amongst staff groups and that

two members of staff in particular were causing problems, possibly because of their own illnesses. (Camden, p. 64)

At Nye Bevan there were other types of disputes. One care assistant tried to get an officer to stop another care assistant talking noisily about a resident in front of him. Another reported the bad practice of a care assistant to officers and headquarters staff. At times care assistants refused to do what they were asked by officers, sometimes threatening the officers with their influence via unions and with the councillors. There was also dissension among the officer group.

Staff Using Money or Goods Inappropriately. Perhaps I should have used the term 'stealing' in my earlier report because there is a danger in words like 'abuse' of appearing to mitigate the seriousness of the behaviour. Pilfering was frequent at Nye Bevan: residents were sometimes asked to pay for care; money was used to purchase hairdressing supplies which disappeared. Elsewhere I have come across examples when staff used residents' food for their own use.

Current Comment on the Categories of Abuse

Thus far, the accounts have been of staff behaviour towards residents. There is hardly a mention of resident abuse to other residents in the reports covered. Today there is growing evidence of resident abuse to other residents. A recent conference on abuse of residents in residential care and nursing homes at Lancaster University (Clough, 1996a) was triggered by the concerns of staff about the sexual abuse of residents by *a male resident* (Osborne, 1996). The male resident had been sexually molesting and assaulting female residents. His behaviour had been known to some staff for several years, but his behaviour was not stopped. Some staff did not know what to do; others raised the matter and found that no action was taken. There is no doubt that residents have immense impact on the lives of other residents. When is such behaviour to be described as *abuse?* When do staff have a responsibility to intervene? Further studies are needed regarding the extent of resident abuse of residents.

One of the ways in which residents intervene in the lives of others is in *improper influence on their behaviour,* a further category that I would now add. The category above, *too authoritarian a life style,* is more about a regime. The element I want to describe in this new category is that of one person going too far in offering advice or comment so that the other does not do what she/he wants. Stevenson (1996) writes of the power exerted by one female resident who controlled the activities of others in the lounge where she sat by telling them things like, 'You don't want to keep getting up and going to the toilet. Sit down!' The resident got up and sat down several times and eventually wet herself. Similarly, staff may 'persuade' or 'encourage' people not to stay in their rooms or to join in activities; there is a fine line between proper interest in the other with concern for their welfare and what becomes an imposition.

Another neglected feature, and hardly apparent in the reports studied, is residents' abuse of staff. The one aspect mentioned at both Nye Bevan and Camden is that black staff were subject to racial abuse from white residents. We know little about the extent of such abuse nor of other unacceptable ways in which residents speak to staff. In addition, staff may be physically or sexually assaulted by residents. Since staff are employed 'to care,' it is difficult for them and their managers to work out the extent to which they should tolerate such behaviour from residents.

The reference to sexual abuse by a male resident at the start of this section alerts us to this aspect of abuse that probably has been under reported or under investigated: sexual abuse. There is minimal information on the sexual abuse of residents even in terms of clear descriptions of the types of events.

Comments in the Reports

All the reports comment on the reasons why the scandal has been allowed to happen. They consider also the process by which the events were revealed and the call for the enquiry or report. Nearly always there is a call to learn from them. In some the combination of appalling events and the knowledge that at least some of them were known for a long time leave the reader bemused as to why nothing was done earlier. I turn first to the explanations offered in the reports.

Explanations

I grouped the various explanations for malpractice found in the reports under the following headings:

1. Failure of different groups to agree about purpose and task.
2. Failure to manage life in the centre in an appropriate way.

3. Resources–buildings and staff.
4. Confusion and lack of knowledge about guidelines.
5. Attitudes and behaviour of staff.
6. Staff capacity and lack of training.
7. Low staff morale.
8. Low status ascribed to the work.
9. Failure to see a pattern in events.

More recently I have termed the three major explanations *structural, environmental,* and *individual characteristic:*

Structural. Older people are held in low esteem and receive poor services. There is little concern with the welfare of older people; indeed, the low status of older people in general will be compounded for those who are dependent on others for care.

Environmental. The environments, in which dependent adults live and in which carers undertake care, create stresses that are intolerable: this affects the behaviour of adult and carer, which leads to abuse.

Individual Characteristic. People with particular personality types or with particular histories (perhaps of being out of control or of being abused by others) are more likely to abuse than others (Clough, 1996b, p. 6).

There is some coherence, and therefore attraction, in this framework. It allows the placing of an individual (with particular characteristics) in her or his immediate environment (the resources available in terms of buildings, facilities, and staff; the nature of the work environment), which in turn exists within a wider societal framework (the views that are held of the worth of older people).

On reflection, there is a danger that elements are missed or not properly emphasised in the middle (environmental) of these levels. It is imperative that this category includes aspects related to staffing, management, and approach to the task. There is potential to consider environmental factors as related more to what is given (numbers of staff, types of buildings, and facilities) rather than the response of staff to their environment.

The aspect which is not given sufficient emphasis is that of the behaviour of staff and managers: their response to circumstances. In considering the influences on an individual's health, recognition is given to three: genetics (the individual inheritance); environment (factors such as air quality, cleanliness of water, levels of radiation), and life-style (the ways in which an individual chooses to live). It is the third of these elements, life style, that provides a clue to the potential missing factor in my categorisation above: *the response of individuals, staff groups, and managers.* Thus I would now add a fourth category, *work style,* to include elements related to staffing and management styles: the failure to agree about purpose and task, the failure to manage in an appropriate way, confusion and lack of knowledge about staffing, and the behaviour of staff. It is inevitable that categories create questions as to boundaries: for example in this framework whether staff capacity and lack of training is categorized as an individual characteristic, environment, or work style item. The key to the use of categories is the relationship between factors rather than what goes into which box.

It is important to recognise the impact of different ways of examining the causation of abuse. For example, explanations related to structures imply that it is society and its approach to the worth of people in a capitalist system that must change; those related to environment stress the necessity for more staff or better buildings; while the individual characteristic explanation allows the idea that it is types of people who abuse. Almost invariably the individual considering the matter will not consider that he or she is the type of person that has the capacity to harm others. I have no doubt that abuse is a consequence of interplay between factors, that given sufficient stress people have a greater capacity to abuse others than they would want to acknowledge, and that the inclusion of a *work style* category encourages consideration of individual and group response to internal and external factors. There are substantial dangers in pursuing a single approach to causation.

Failure to Manage

The Camden Report highlights factors pertinent to the quality of care with poor care practices becoming entrenched and employment practices, designed to protect staff, leading to failure to discipline. The influence of the officer in charge (OIC) is stressed in several of the reports studied, including Nye Bevan. The enquiry came to the conclusion that 'the brunt of the responsibility for the situation at NBL (Nye Bevan Lodge) must lie squarely at the feet of the OIC' (Gibbs, Evans, & Rodway, 1987, p. 78). However *failure to manage* should be taken to include external management's responsibility, together with its relationship with the internal manager. The task of management is to translate the understanding of what should happen into what does happen, coupled with taking action when matters are seen to be unsatisfactory. Both the Camden and Nye Bevan reports show that much of the information available to the enquiries had been known in various ways to managers. When the information is presented in the enquiry reports, it is difficult to understand why people did not act. It is to that which I now turn.

Revelation

In some of the child care establishments there had been protests of different types by groups of residents. Although comparatively unusual in children's homes and schools, there is no evidence of these acts in homes for older people. Complaints typically are made to someone's confidantes: relatives, other friends, or particular staff. The action of a resident at Nye Bevan is very unusual. '. . . (He) went to the Town Hall and said that he wanted to leave Nye Bevan Lodge because it was like a concentration camp (he had been in one during the war)' (Gibbs, Evans, & Rodway, 1987, p. 27).

An enquiry is called when external managers or outsiders determine that the only way to form a view of what happened *and* to start to restore confidence in the integrity of staff and the quality of the practice is to appoint someone independent with recognised competence in the field or in conducting investigations.

I suggested in the Wagner paper that one of the reasons why action was not taken earlier was a failure to see a pattern in events.

> Three different examples of this arise in the Nye Bevan report. Firstly, the history of the care assistant who became drunk was not compiled to give an over-view of her work; secondly, an inappropriate pattern was imposed (on the data) that distorted what was actually happening (alcoholism was viewed in Southwark as a sickness and the consequence for the capacity to care were forgotten); thirdly, '. . . the SMT (senior management team) tended to view matters in isolation and failed to recognise that each incident was but a part of a pattern which they should have identified and dealt with.' (Clough, 1988, p. 39)

There is abundant evidence in child protection literature of the consequences of failing to stand back and to take an overview, in part because staff have been so wedded to their own view of what was happening that they did not want to open events to comment from others. In residential care, mangers may want to deal with events in particular ways *as isolated events.*

A further explanation is one with which I have become more aware following work in registration and inspection: the records which would allow a study of other events may not have been kept. There is a tension between the interests of staff and those of residents. In terms of personnel practice it seems reasonable that staff who are subject to internal disciplinary procedures in which findings of guilt are not proven or dismissed should have the record expunged from their file. Indeed, in an increasingly litigious environment this becomes of greater importance. Yet, not keeping records of earlier proceedings means that, at a later stage investigation, no records are available that will show a pattern of concern. I can see no alternative other than that staff working in direct care should accept the fact that confidential records of all enquiries into their practice are maintained.

An important component in analysing abuse (and in combatting it) is degrees of openness. The events which are later termed as abuse may or may not have been kept secret within the establishment. In residential child care there are examples of activities that later are judged to be abusive, not only not being hidden but presented as part of the practice style: at an extreme, abuse is presented as therapy. I know of no direct parallel in residential care of older people though there are some similarities in management of residents' behaviour which staff or other residents find problematic. Thus it is not uncommon (though not part of the Camden or Southwark enquiries) for residents to have been tied to chairs or even not allowed to go outside because staff did not know what else to do for their or others' welfare.

The second pattern is one where there is an expectation that the events will be kept secret; in whatever way the actions are presented, the presumption is that they will not be talked about openly and that they will not be seen by others. People keep things to themselves for a number of reasons: fear; shame; concern that others will be contaminated; ignorance of their rights or that what is being done to them is wrong or illegal, even though they may dislike it; misplaced loyalty; and doubts that they will be believed and anybody will do anything.

Examining Doubts

One difficulty for people who are concerned about practices is knowing how to interpret the information they have. In determining what to do people, in effect, ask themselves how worried they should be about the events. Such doubts may lead people to do nothing, and it is clear that doing nothing on one occasion makes it harder to do something on other occasions. In the Wagner study I suggested that it would be useful to compile a list of factors that might help in the interpretation of events. Such *predisposing* factors could act like alarm bells. Drawing on material from outside those reports my current list of factors which should be considered in interpreting individual events is:

- Previous complaints: number, time-scale, numbers of staff;
- Establishment appears run down: this relates to the general standards of maintenance and also to the day to day attention that is given to the building;
- Staffing: levels of shortages and sickness; high turnover; little supervision, in particular at night; high consumption of alcohol;
- Senior staff: absent, uninterested, preoccupied with events in their own lives; in post for a very long time;
- Residents: few visitors; rarely go out; regarded as highly demanding, awkward or problematic; their demeanour and response to staff;
- Uncertainty about the future of the establishment;
- Staff attitude and behaviour towards residents;
- Discord among staff team.

I have no doubt that a critical component in reducing the potential for abuse is to create an environment in which openness is encouraged and staff are expected to talk about their uncertainties about practice, whether their own or those of others. The same applies to residents and visitors. The first and overriding loyalty is to the well being of residents. The critical test is whether an individual would be happy if the practice were to happen to him or her, or to her or his parents.

Direct Care

I ended my earlier report with a comment on the characteristics of residential work and management. I conclude this article with a consideration of the task which I now term direct care. The direct care of others involves varying degrees of intimacy in personal care: staff are directly doing things to, with, and for residents. There is no model for this type of work, and it is difficult for staff to comprehend the components: authority, boundaries, intimacy, for example. Staff need to have a vision of what they should be doing and how to manage when under pressure. Against what model, values, or code of practice are they to judge their own or others' work?

Without a framework the task itself may take precedence and the reasons for the task are forgotten. For example, there may be a 'drive to complete,' anxiety when residents do not do what is suggested, or uncertainty as to responsibility when residents are behaving badly towards others. For example, as an SSD inspector I had evidence of an officer in charge trying to persuade some older people that it was time to go to bed and they refused. The officer's husband picked them up and carried or dragged them to bed. Staff frequently are faced with decisions as to whether residents should be able to leave the home: they have no formal powers to restrict them; yet relatives and members of the public expect the residents to be kept safe. Further, the staff themselves may be concerned for the welfare of the residents. The tension is apparent.

Many writers on residential work highlight the importance of management, leadership style, and cohesion amongst the staff team (Wolins, 1982; Clough, 1982; Brown & Clough, 1989) mirroring what is written about in industry (e.g., Peters & Waterman, 1982). The complexity and responsibility of direct care needs to be recognised. Highlighted in the study (Clough, 1996) is the importance of directors of social services believing in the value of residential care if a social services department is to run its own homes.

Structural factors influence the climate in which abuse takes place. Such abuse of people who expect care is appalling and frightening. Closing our eyes to what happens because the events are unpalatable will help only to perpetuate bad practice and abuse. We have to build on current knowledge to create places in which structures, environment, appointed staff, and the work styles they adopt all make abuse less likely and its early detection more certain.

REFERENCES

Camden (1987). *A report into Camden's residential homes.* London: Camden County Council.

Clough, R. (1982). *Residential work.* London: BASW/Macmillan.

Clough, R. (1988). *Scandals in residential centres: A report to the Wagner Committee.* Unpublished.

Clough, R. (ed.) (1994). *Insights into inspection: The regulation of social care.* London: Whiting and Birch.

Clough, D. (1996). Uncovering abuse. In Clough R. (1996a).

Clough, R. (ed.) (1996a). *The abuse of care in residential institutions.* London: Whiting and Birch.

Clough, R. (1996b). The abuse of care: The person and the place. In Clough R. (1996a).

Clough, R. (1996c). The abuse of older people in residential and nursing homes. *Nursing Times Review,* 1: 6.

Gibbs, J., Evans M. & Rodway, S. (1987). *Report of the inquiry into Nye Bevan Lodge.* London: London Borough of Southwark Social Services Department.

Osborne, J. (1996). Managing enquiries. In Clough R. (ed.) (1996a).

Peters, T. & Waterman R. (1982). *In search of excellence.* New York: Harper and Row.

Stevenson, O. (1996). Issues for further reflection. In Clough R. (1996a).

Wagner Committee (1988). *Residential care: A positive choice report of the independent review of residential care,* Vol. 1. London: HMSO.

Wolins, M. (1982). *Revitalising residential settings.* California: Jossey Bass.

Visibility Blues:
Gender Issues in Elder Abuse
in Institutional Settings

Gabriele Griffin, PhD
Lynda Aitken, MA

SUMMARY. This article argues that elder abuse in institutional as opposed to domestic settings remains invisible because institutions for elders are mainly all-female spaces where ageism and sexism converge and clients and workers are economically and socially disadvantaged. A general culture of violence that increasingly legitimates the everydayness of abuse and that conforms to dominant gender stereotypes refuses to investigate abuse of women by women. Research is needed into the different kinds of abuse committed in institutional settings by women. Staff and clients need to be enabled to report abuse and effective measures for combating it put in place. *[Article copies available for a fee from The Haworth Document Delivery Service: 1-800-342-9678. E-mail address: getinfo@haworthpressinc.com]*

KEYWORDS. Elder abuse, gender, institutional settings, paid carers, financial abuse, violence

INTRODUCTION

Little research had been done on elder abuse in institutional settings in contrast to such abuse in domestic contexts (e.g., Eastman, 1984;

Gabriele Griffin is Professor of Women's Studies, Leeds Metropolitan University, Calverley Street, Leeds LS1 3HE, UK. (Email: g-griffin@mu.ac.uk). Lynda Aitken is Unit Manager, Danetree Lodge, Danetree Hospital, Daventry, Northants, UK.

[Haworth co-indexing entry note]: "Visibility Blues: Gender Issues in Elder Abuse in Institutional Settings." Griffin, Gabriele, and Lynda Aitken. Co-published simultaneously in *Journal of Elder Abuse & Neglect* (The Haworth Maltreatment & Trauma Press, an imprint of The Haworth Press, Inc.) Vol. 10, No. 1/2, 1999, pp. 29-42; and: *Elder Abuse and Neglect in Residential Settings: Different National Backgrounds and Similar Responses* (ed: Frank Glendenning, and Paul Kingston) The Haworth Press, Inc., 1999, pp. 29-42. Single or multiple copies of this article are available for a fee from The Haworth Document Delivery Service [1-800-342-9678, 9:00 a.m. - 5:00 p.m. (EST). E-mail address: getinfo@ haworthpressinc.com].

Steinmetz, 1988; Decalmer & Glendenning, 1993, 1997; McCreadie, 1993): hence the title of this article, 'Visibility Blues.' Elder abuse in institutional settings is not very visible. Most of the evidence for such abuse comes through investigative journalism like Catherine Bennett's (1994) report or through reports of court cases such as the notorious Nye Bevan Lodge case (Gibbs, 1987). Cases involving criminal pro-ceedings are rare in the UK. In this article we therefore want to examine why elder abuse in institutional settings remains invisible, with a particular emphasis on the following issues:

1. Prevalence;
2. The gendered specificity of elder abuse in institutional settings with regard to clients and workers;
3. The economics of care;
4. The culture of violence we inhabit;
5. Issues of agency and dependence; and
6. Problems with intervention.

ISSUES OF PREVALENCE

One reason for the invisibility of elder abuse in institutional settings may be its low level of prevalence. Aronson (1990) maintains: 'It is estimated that . . . 'informal care' of the elderly constitutes 90% of the total care provided in society, the remaining 10% being supplied by the formal health and social services' (p. 62). Brindle (1996) points out that 'In mid-1986, there were fewer than 190,000 places in pri-vate and voluntary homes; by the middle of 1995, there were 440,000' (p. 2). With the rise in the number of institutions for elders in the private sector in the UK following the implementation of the National Health Service and Community Care Act in 1993, opportuni-ties for abuse have increased, in part because that sector is largely unregulated. While these figures are likely to shift, they nonetheless suggest that institutional abuse may not be as extensive a problem as domestic abuse simply because fewer elders are in institutions than at home. Glendenning (1993: 1) maintains that about five per cent of older people in Britain and in the USA live in institutional care. He views these people as more at risk of abuse than the 95% living in the community but offers no further information to support his claims–an index of the invisibility of such abuse. However, the Action on Elder

Abuse's (1997a) evaluation of their pilot helpline project found that one quarter of perpetrators in cases of abuse reported to their helpline were said to be a paid care worker and that, while 70% of reported abuse occurred in the victim's own home, 27.5% occurred in various residential settings from nursing homes to hospitals (p. 2). Three times as many women as men were reported to be victims. Many more live in privately run homes or occupy hospital beds, but no figures are available on these. The gender difference indicated here is consistent throughout all types of residential care. Given then that nearly three times as many women as men are in residential care, older women are more likely to be the objects of abuse in residential settings than men. However, as regards prevalence of elder abuse in institutional settings, we are actually still very much in the dark. This should not induce complacency; Stevenson (1989) maintains that 'there is little point in wasting research time on the incidence of old age abuse' (p. 22), arguing for the need to raise levels of awareness on the part of professionals and a willingness to entertain the possibility that it exists instead. It has to be recognised that the government, including, disappointingly, the new Labour government in the UK, has little incentive to invest in such research as the privatization of care has been one of its ways of dealing with the increasing needs for care in our population.

THE GENDERED SPECIFICITY OF ELDER ABUSE IN INSTITUTIONAL SETTINGS

A further reason why so little is known about elder abuse in institutional settings is that the latter constitute a predominantly female world, in that both the clients and the workers in institutions for elders are in the main women. Most elder abuse is meted out to people in their 70s and 80s (Aitken & Griffin, 1996). The vast majority of over 74-year-olds are women (*Women of Europe*, 1997: 5). Most workers in homes for elders are women, often untrained and always poorly paid. But, as is the case in other abuse situations such as child sexual abuse and domestic violence, discussions of institutional care and abuse tend to mask the gender specificities pertinent to that situation. Hilary Brown and Helen Smith (1993) have commented on the ways in which the 1990s rhetoric of care invisibilized its gendered implications. The 'reality' of elder abuse occurring in institutions devoted to the care of older people is that a predominantly female workforce abuses a predominantly female client group (Jack, 1994: 78). But there is little willingness either to acknowledge or to analyse this situation.

Abusing Women

The abuse of women by women remains under-researched because it violates socio-cultural expectations of role distributions and behaviours for women and men which construct women as non-abusive and men as abusive. Typically, female violence, for example, is regarded as the expression of someone who is either 'mad' or 'bad.' In dominant discourse, violence between women is frequently read in the light of inter-sexual relations, i.e., the woman is violent because she is enthralled to a 'bad' man (what one might call the Myra Hindley syndrome–Myra Hindley is a notorious child murderer) or she is acting out a revenge for being spurned by a man (as presented in the film *Fatal Attraction*), or she is simply in and of herself dysfunctional, i.e., 'mad' (the explanation in the Beverly Allitt case in England). Here the focus of the enquiry tends to be on the individual woman who is presented as an exception to the norm; structural inequalities which might contribute to her behaviour are ignored in order to establish her deviance as 'not the norm' as far as women in general are concerned. Thus, the maintenance of the status quo as regards gender stereotyping takes precedence over an investigation of structural inequalities and of gender roles that might reveal the inadequacies of the norms so extensively taken for granted in explanations of female behaviour.

One typical example of this in the context of elder abuse was reported in a local newspaper in Northampton in June 1992 when a nurse manager who ran a private home 'roughly dragged a senile seventy year old woman, yanking off her underwear, calling her a 'filthy pig' and slapped her' ('Bully nurse escapes ban,' *Northampton Chronicle* and *Echo*, 6 June 1992, p. 4). She consistently verbally and physically abused elders in her care. The nurse had previously (1987) been convicted of common assault, but it had then taken five years before her case came before the Nurses Professional Conduct Committee. The nurse was found guilty of misconduct but her name was not struck from the nurses' register ('Bully nurse escapes ban,' 1992). The nurse's solicitor argued that 'she suffered extreme duress from her violent and tortuous marriage'–the story of the abused abusing. The nurse's victimisation by her husband was used to explain her abuse of others. On one level, this (reassuringly) reduced her behaviour to the level of the unfortunate individual who acts in response to her own violation. The nurse was thus cast, as women often are, as a 'victim,' an object, who did not intentionally commit abuse but responded to being abused. This affirms dominant stereotypes of femininity, thus retrieving the status quo of gender roles threatened by her behaviour. The containment of her having been abused within the domestic sphere, i.e., her marriage, suggests not only an 'accepted' pattern of inter-gender violence but also indicates the boundaries of the abusive scenario: the 'home.' The issue of the ways in which the construction of certain kinds of residential settings for elders as 'home from home' also brings with it the attendant problems of the privatisation of the domestic space. The resultant legitimisation of abuse within this context needs to be researched.

THE ECONOMICS OF CARE

Older women are notoriously devalued in our culture (Arber & Ginn, 1995; Hugman, 1994). Ageism and sexism converge to create a situation of invisibility that has been much discussed elsewhere (e.g., Mahoney, 1994; Norman, 1985; Stevenson, 1989). As Aronson (1990) points out in relation to older women dealing with service providers: 'many were acutely attuned to their devalued status as old women' (p. 69). But invisibility also pertains to the female staff in homes for elders. Thus there is little professional status attached to working with elders (Treharne, 1990: 777), not only because those who do so are women and women's work is habitually devalued but also because the work supposedly does not demand skilled labour and is poorly paid (Brown & Smith, 1993). The result may be financial abuse by financially hard pressed workers of financially impoverished elders. *Community Care* (1996) reported the case of a care assistant who 'stole from elderly residents . . . because . . . she was living in poverty' (Anonymous: 7). Aitken (Aitken & Griffin, 1996) found that such abuse was routine and went unquestioned.

The distinction commonly made between formal, that is *paid*, and informal, i.e., *unpaid* care, reflects the economically driven ideology that informs care of elders. Paid carers are economically victimised in our culture (Rickford, 1996). The assumption that women care because they are nurturant, implicitly encoded in many contemporary care proposals, etc., (Brown & Smith, 1993) is in direct conflict with the fact that for many women caring is–quite legitimately–'just a job.' The women working as care assistants or home helps, for example, should not be assumed to be working in order to do some 'labour of love' (Finch & Groves, 1983) but do so because they need to survive on the money they get. As Kappeler (1995: 27) writes: 'so-called selflessness can become rational self-interest, namely the means by which to realise the advantages (however meagre) that patriarchal society offers to women.' In her view 'the deprivation of women in patriarchy consists not in the loss of self through self-sacrifice, but in the lack of political rights and material opportunities to survive and exist other than through the labour of 'love' and care.'

Paid carers' relationship to their 'charges' is an overtly economic one. As one woman nursing home manager said: 'Staff-wise you get some that are not so good–it shouldn't be like that, but you're talking economics' (Bennett, 1994, p. 14). Residential and nursing homes employ women in terms of the institution's economic 'needs' rather than to ensure the best possible care for their clients. Kappeler (1995) discusses the prevalence of economistic terminology in current descriptions of all kinds of different relationships, suggesting that with this vocabulary comes an attitude which privileges 'value for money,' 'exchange value,' etc. She maintains that the use of economic metaphors serves to transform relations of potential equality into ones of domination and submission in cases where the exchange seems unequal. In the case of service providers such as carers on low pay, the question of what these women get out of doing their work is an important one. In a climate in which equivalence of return is the dominant expectation, being asked to do a physically, and potentially emotionally, demanding job without a sense that an equivalent return (possibly, but not inevitably, in pecuniary form) is offered, may lead –at least in some people–to a need to seek other kinds of recompense. These can include the pleasure of power over others, exercised through not responding to their needs, for example. Residential and nursing homes, while needing their clients to exist, are nonetheless sites of inequality where the dependence of the clients on the staff's support is matched only by the staff's need to earn a living but where the living earned is extremely small compared to the work required.

Such disequilibrium in an economically driven ideological climate provides a seed bed for abuse.

THE CULTURE OF VIOLENCE:
AGENCY AND OBJECTIFICATION

This potential for abuse is further enhanced by the culture we live in that condones much of the violence and violation that occurs within it. Elder abuse involves an act of violation (of whatever kind) perpetrated by the abuser against the abused. Such acts may be differentially motivated across diverse situations but they are fed by what Kappeler describes as a culture which endorses violence through its 'primary identification with the subjects of violence and our lack of solidarity with the victims. [This] is itself an act of violence: the exercise of ideological violence, of the power of the discourse which legitimates violence, stigmatises the victims, and treats people not as agents of their own actions but as material for ('our') social policy' (Kappeler, 1995: 7). In other words, those who act violently are 'excused' by pointing to conditions which may promote violence and which need changing rather than by considering their responsibility as individuals for their actions. This position is evident in some feminists' (e.g., Ungerson, 1987)–including our own–and others' tendency to identify with the plight of the carer and to see themselves as potential carers, that is as subjects in control of the action, rather than acknowledging the possibility that they might need care and thereby become the objects of caregiving. Kappeler maintains that the structures of thought and argumentation which legitimate violence in Western culture and inform our actions are so 'deeply rooted in our everyday thinking' that they inform all our behaviour:

> What is remarkable is that this everyday behaviour, in so far as it does not fall within the competence of criminal law, is hardly the subject of a serious theoretical discussion. Neither does it attract explicit legitimation; rather, the violence of everyday behaviour draws its legitimacy from the ubiquity of such behaviour in our society and the social consensus about its relative 'harmlessness' compared with other, that is recognized forms of violence. (Kappeler, 1995: 7)

This situation relates directly to a key point made by Margaret Kennedy at the 'Violence, Abuse and Women's Citizenship' conference (November 1996, Brighton) that in an increasingly violent society in which representations of violence, for example, show more and more extreme forms of violence we–as a consequence–fail to recognise and/or respond to lesser forms of violence. But violence is not the only form of elder abuse; other forms are present and tolerated. A good example of this was the generalised acceptance by the social workers Aitken interviewed (Aitken & Griffin, 1996) of financial abuse of elders that appeared to be ubiqutous and routine. This state of affairs is very worrisome especially given that older women, due to the post-war history of taxation and pension regimes, are often very poorly off financially (Groves, 1992; *Women of Europe*, 1997), then too, their poverty is compounded by inadequate advice about the financial contributions they have to make towards their care (MacErlean, 1997). The underlying attitude of legitimation of such abuse, implicit in the failure to intervene, contributes to its invisibility.

DEPENDENCY, POWER, AND CONTROL
IN INSTITUTIONAL ABUSE

Women (and men) enter institutional care as a last resort as opposed to a first choice (Hugman, 1994: 128), with the degree of dependency on intensive and sustained levels of care often being crucial in the transition from domestic to institutional care (Ross, Rosenthal, & Dawson, 1993: 1533). In contemporary Western culture, dependency is negatively constructed as the opposite of autonomy, not dissimilar to the opposition between victim and perpetrator or object and subject. As Mahoney (1994) puts it: 'Agency–acting for oneself–is generally seen as an individual matter, the functioning of an atomistic, mobile individual' (p. 60). An older woman in need of extended care can–within these terms–clearly not be regarded as possessing agency and the assumption, on entry into a caring institution (note the irony of the phrase), tends to be that the older woman has relinquished agency. This reduction of older women's agency once they enter a home is reinforced by territorial issues that come into play in any institution and that are enacted through daily routines and regimes, many of which are, or verge on, abusive. One of the best known but least attended to phenomena of abuse in institutions is the batch treatment meted out to the clients that includes all kinds of restrictive regimes. These are imposed on older people regarding even the most basic of their functions, from when they are 'allowed' to eat or drink, to when they are toileted, whom they can share a room with or have in their room, what personal possessions they can bring, etc. Such regimes are standard both in state run and in privately owned homes, reinforcing the idea that on entering the caring institution, the older woman loses her individuality and decision-making powers in favour of becoming an institutional unit. As Blank, Levesque, and Winter (1993) put it:

> An institution is generally a bad place for elderly persons to exert or desire direct, overt control . . . because the institutions run most smoothly when the elderly are passive recipients of care from the staff; that is, when the distribution of control activity is almost totally in the direction of the staff, and staff are in control of the allocation of control by the nature of the setting. In such situations, a strong desire for control will go unquenched; actual control attempts will be met with resistance. (Blank, Levesque & Winter, 1993: 279)

Bennett (1994) provides an example of this from her visits to nursing homes for elders. At one point, 'In one corridor a woman was poised between a chair and a Zimmer frame, struggling to heave herself upright. As we passed her, the manager placed her hand on the woman's shoulders and without comment, forced her back into the chair' (Bennett, 1994: 12). Here impairment and institutionalisation contribute to the objectification and victimisation of the older woman who is acted upon without explanation or recourse to redress. Ageism and sexism converge in this situation of dependency to result in the objectification of that woman and in the 'freedom'–even in front of an 'outsider'–to abuse her. The very fact of the abuse, of course, reinforces the power differential between the older woman and the abusing matron and thus serves to perpetuate it. Another form of abuse is over-medication and sedation (Hirst, 1997), frequently used and considered acceptable in institutions for elders, particularly where dementia is involved (Alzheimer's Disease Society, 1997).

PROBLEMS WITH INTERVENTION

The preceding examples raise the issue of different kinds and degrees of abuse. At present, as the Action on Elder Abuse's (1997b) leaflet, *Elder abuse in care homes: What to do and who to contact* makes clear, elder abuse is treated as a unitary concept. The leaflet states: 'Abuse may be physical, psychological, financial or sexual. Wilful neglect can also be a type of abuse.' Most of the cases of abuse reported and responded to are, in fact, physical (Phillipson, 1992; SSI, 1992), presumably because these leave visible marks. But abuse comes in many guises and, as Nazroo's (1995) work on intra-marital violence has shown, we need to distinguish the impact and effect of abuse by women from that of abuse by men. Additionally, and importantly, research needs to be carried out into the differences between abuse in *institutional* as opposed to domestic settings. Certain kinds of abuse such as batch treatment are specific to institutional settings and can be a function of under-staffing and/or poor staff training. Different types of abuse clearly require different kinds of intervention. This pertains, inter alia, to situations where visitors, such as relatives, to residential settings who (continue to) abuse those in the home are the perpetrators of abuse.

Much of the writing on problems about control, power, and institutions assumes that those institutionalised are in a position to act on their own behalf in situations of abuse. However, high degrees of dependency which may be the result of physical and/or mental decline are not necessarily conducive to putting up a fight. Quite apart from the anxiety about who would care for oneself if one were to accuse the institution and caring individuals within it of abuse, there is the difficulty of whom to turn to and what to say–provided the older person is in a state to make such claims (Francis, 1993).

These circumstances are exacerbated by the inadequate inspection system that prevails. Bennett (1994) observed routine violations of the 1984 'code of practice called Home Life . . . published by the DHSS . . . the principal source of guidance on the residential care of the elderly' (Bennett, 1994: 12) when she visited nursing homes for elders. In the UK there are no overall national guidelines for the inspection of nursing homes (Bennett, 1994: 18). They are registered and inspected by the health authority. Residential homes are inspected by Social Services. The inspection units of both the health authority and social service departments are often over stretched, and although they can close a home, the action taken by courts and professional bodies against workers found guilty of abuse is indicative of the low regard accorded older people and does not encourage reporting abuse. For instance: Dumfries and Galloway Social Services Department managers were found to be complacent and inept in failing to identify and rectify the brutal regime of a matron at a residential home over a twenty-year period. She was found unfit to plead at her trial on thirty-one charges of cruelty. Despite the recommendations of the enquiry, the home was not closed by the local authorities (S.W.D. Found Guilty, 1993: 2). There have been calls to end the dual inspection system and discussions are currently under way but 'most practitioners predict homes will end up with less regulation rather than more' (White, 1997).

Even where there is evidence of abuse, action does not necessarily follow. Staff may not be prepared to whistle blow because they need their jobs and stand to lose them if homes are closed down as the result of a complaint. Insecurity of employment can breed silence and collusion (White, 1997). Staff, especially casual untrained staff, may also not know what to do. Oxford describes the case of an 82-year old woman, obviously mistreated and possibly sexually abused (indexed by repeated vaginal infections and 'unexplained bruises on her upper legs') by a younger man. Both home helps and social workers were aware of the situation but 'Helpers look on, frustrated and afraid for her. There is little they can do.' The difficulty is that 'There is no coherent legal framework designed to protect old people' (Oxford, 1995: 21). Additionally, solutions may not always be straightforward. This is compounded by the 'learned helplessness' among the helping professions as a phenomenon which occurs when a systematic lack of resources gives rise to the inability of professionals to meet the needs of [abused] women, resulting in the erosion of hope and initiative among professionals' (Mahoney, 1994: 64).

Relatives may have nothing to judge standards by and may simply do nothing. In a headline-making case, a carer described how her elderly mother who suffered from Alzheimer's disease went into the hospital for respite care but 'came out covered in bruises and bedsores, and it took us weeks to [get] her back to normal.' Although the carer 'couldn't understand how she could come out in such a terrible state when she was being looked after by people who were professionally trained to care' (Rickford, 1996: 2), she clearly did nothing to pursue this situation.

CONCLUSIONS

We live in a culture that endorses violence as everyday behaviour to such an extent that everyday violence becomes invisible. Much of this violence is directed against women and some of it is carried out by women. Our culture promotes autonomy rather than dependence, with the consequence that those who act as subjects–the perpetrators of abuse–are identified with rather than their victims, the objects of such abuse. The extent of the expectation of such an identification was made clear in Bennett's (1994) report detailed above in which one matron did obviously not feel in the least compromised by how she was treating an older woman in her care in front of a third person who supposedly was contemplating putting one of her older relations into that home. In consequence, little is done when elder abuse in institutional settings occurs. This inaction is also associated with the fact that both female workers and clients in institutions for elders suffer from low social and economic status which 'legitimates' their neglect of both groups. We have yet to acknowledge properly that:

- the vast majority of workers and clients in institutions for elders are women;
- institutionally based elder abuse is therefore predominantly of women by women;
- these women are socially and economically disempowered;
- there are power differences between female workers and female clients by virtue of their respective intra-institutional in/ability to determine their daily lives;
- institutions for elders foster abuse through a variety of direct and indirect means, including the regimes and hierarchy that exist within them;
- there is a need to investigate the differences between domestic and institutionally-based elder abuse;
- research into the different kinds/degrees of abuse committed by women is needed;
- workers may not know how to identify abuse or deal with it when they encounter it; and
- the government has little incentive to investigate elder abuse in institutional settings as it relies on these settings to implement its funds-starved policies.

REFERENCES

Action on Elder Abuse (1997a). *Hearing the despair: The reality of elder abuse.* London: Action on Elder Abuse.

Action on Elder Abuse (1997b). *Elder abuse in care homes: What to do and who to contact.* London: Action on Elder Abuse.

Aitken, L. & Griffin, G. (1996). *Gender issues in elder abuse.* London: Sage.

Alzheimer's Disease Society (1997). *Experience of care in residential and nursing homes.* London: Alzheimer's Disease Society.

Aronson, J. (1990). Women's perspectives on informal care of the elderly: Public ideology and personal experience of giving and receiving care. *Ageing and Society*, 10, 61-84.

Anon. (1996). Court fines care assistant for theft. *Community Care*, 5-11 September, 7.

Arber, S. & Ginn, J. (eds). (1995) *Connecting gender and ageing.* Buckingham: Open University Press.

Bennett, C. (1994). Ending up. *The Guardian Weekend*, 8 October, 12-14, 18, 20.

Blank, T. O., Levesque, M. J. & Winter, G. P. (1993). The triad of control: Concepts and applications to caregiving. *International Journal of Behavioral Development*, 16(2), 261-86.

Brindle, D. (1996). The shame of growing old. *The Guardian*, 16 October, 2-3.

Brown, H. & Smith, H. (1993). Women caring for people: The mismatch between rhetoric and women's reality? *Policy and Politics*, 21(3), 185-93.

Bully Nurse Escapes Ban (1992). *Northampton Chronicle and Echo*, 6 June, 4.

Eastman, M. (1984). *Old age abuse.* London: Age Concern.

Finch, J. & Groves, D. (eds.) (1983). *A Labour of love: Women, work and caring.* London: Routledge and Kegan Paul.

Francis, J. (1993). Where do you draw the line? *Community Care*, 20 May, 18-19.

Gibbs, J. et al. (1987). *Report of the enquiry into Nye Bevan Lodge.* London: Borough of Southwark.

Decalmer, P. & Glendenning, F. (eds.) (1993, 1997). *The Mistreatment of elderly people.* London: Sage Publications.

Glendenning, F. (1993, 1997). What is elder abuse and neglect? In Decalmer, P. & Glendenning, F. (eds.), *The mistreatment of elderly people.* London: Sage, 1-34 (1st edn.); 13-41 (2nd edn.).

Groves, D. (1992). Occupational pension provision and women's poverty in old age. In Glendinning, C. & Millar, J. (eds.), *Women and poverty in Britain–the 1990s.* Hemel Hempstead: Harvester Wheatsheaf, 176-92.

Hirst, J. (1997). Twilight zones. *Community Care*, 22-28 May, 12.

Hugman, R. (1994). *Ageing and the care of older people in Europe.* Houndsmill: Macmillan.

Jack, R. (1994). Dependence, power and violation: Gender issues in abuse of elderly people by formal carers. In Eastman, M. (ed.), *Old age abuse: A new perspective.* London: Chapman and Hall, 77-92.

Kappeler, S. (1995). *The will to violence: The politics of personal behaviour.* Cambridge: Polity Press.

Kennedy, M. (1996). *From the cradle to the grave: Sexual abuse and violence against disabled women and children.* Unpublished Conference Paper. International Conference on Violence, Abuse and Women's Citizenship, November 1996, Brighton.

MacErlean, N. (1997). Councils' confusion on care. *The Observer*, 1 June, 16.

McCreadie, C. (1993). *Elder abuse: New findings and policy guidelines.* London: Age Concern Institute of Gerontology.

Mahoney, M. R. (1994). Victimization or oppression? Women's lives, violence, and agency. In Albertson Fineman, M. & Mykitiuk, R. (eds.), *The public nature of private violence.* London: Routledge, 59-92.

Nazroo, J. (1995). Uncovering gender differences in the use of marital violence: The effect of methodology. *Sociology*, 29(3), August, 475-94.

Norman, A. (1985). *Triple jeopardy: Growing old in a second homeland.* London: Centre for Policy on Ageing.

Oxford, E. (1995). Cruelty to elderly people: Do we care? *The Times*, 19 April, 21.

Phillipson, C. (1992). Confronting elder abuse: Fact and fiction. *Generations Review*, 2(3), September, 2-3.

Pillemer, K. A. & Finkelhor, D. (1988). The prevalence of elder abuse: A random survey sample. *The Gerontologist*, 28(1), 51-7.

Rickford, F. (1996). To the victor the losses. *The Guardian*, 17 July, 2.

Ross, M. M., Rosenthal, C. J., & Dawson, P. G. (1993). Spousal caregiving following institutionalization: The experience of elderly wives. *Journal of Advanced Nursing*, 18, 1531-9.

[SSI] Social Services Inspectorate. (1992). *Confronting elder abuse.* London: HMSO.

Steinmetz, S. K. (1988). *Duty bound: Elder abuse and family care.* Sage Library of Social Research. Vol. 166. London: Sage.

Stevenson, O. (1989). *Age and vulnerability: A guide to better care.* London: Edward Arnold.

S.W. D. Found Guilty (1993). *Community Care*, 7 January, 2.

Treharne, G. (1990). Attitudes towards the care of elderly people: Are they getting better? *Journal of Advanced Nursing*, 15, 777-81.

Ungerson, C. (1987). *Policy is personal: Sex, gender and informal care.* London: Tavistock.

White, C. (1997). Abusing the position. *Community Care*, 1-7 February, 30-1.

Women of Europe. (1997). Age becomes her: Older women in the European Union. Dossier 45, May-July, Bruxelles: European Commission.

Elder Abuse
in Residential Settings in Sweden

Britt-Inger Saveman, RNT, PhD
Sture Åström, RNT, DMSc
Gösta Bucht, MD, PhD
Astrid Norberg, RN, PhD

SUMMARY. To investigate frequencies and types of elder abuse occurring in residential settings in two municipal areas of Sweden, nursing staff were asked to answer a questionnaire; 499 responded. The findings indicated that elder abuse involving the staff did occur. Eleven percent of the staff knew of situations of elder abuse and two percent admitted that they themselves had been abusive towards an elderly resident. Psychological and physical abuse related to caring activities were

---

Britt-Inger Saveman is Senior Lecturer, Kalmar University, Department of Caring Sciences and Social Work, Kalmar, Sweden, and is affiliated with the Department of Advanced Nursing, Umeå University, Umeå. Sture Åström is Senior Lecturer, College of Health and Caring Sciences, Umeå, and is affiliated with the Department of Advanced Nursing and Department of Geriatric Medicine, Umeå University, Umeå. Gösta Bucht is Professor, Department of Geriatric Medicine, and Astrid Norberg is Professor, Department of Advanced Nursing, both at Umeå University, Umeå, Sweden.

Address correspondence to: Britt-Inger Saveman, Kalmar University, Department of Caring Sciences and Social Work, Box 905, S-39129 Kalmar, Sweden (E-mail: britt-inger.saveman@vh.hik.se).

The authors would like to thank Mr. Pikka Annela for valuable statistical consultations and Ms. Gullvi Nilsson for revising the English.

This study was supported by the Swedish Foundation for Health Caring Sciences and Allergy Research and Kalmar County Council.

[Haworth co-indexing entry note]: "Elder Abuse in Residential Settings in Sweden." Saveman et al. Co-published simultaneously in *Journal of Elder Abuse & Neglect* (The Haworth Maltreatment & Trauma Press, an imprint of The Haworth Press, Inc.) Vol. 10, No. 1/2, 1999, pp. 43-60; and: *Elder Abuse and Neglect in Residential Settings: Different National Backgrounds and Similar Responses* (ed: Frank Glendenning, and Paul Kingston) The Haworth Press, Inc., 1999, pp. 43-60. Single or multiple copies of this article are available for a fee from The Haworth Document Delivery Service [1-800-342-9678, 9:00 a.m. - 5:00 p.m. (EST). E-mail address: getinfo@haworthpressinc.com].

most common. In the specific situations reported, the abusers were mostly characterised as hot-tempered, exhausted, and burned out. The abused people were often mentally and/or physically handicapped and generally over 80 years old. Feelings such as powerlessness, anger towards the abuser, and compassion for the abused person were reported. To cope with the situation, they talked to each other or to the manager. They recommended more education and support as the main preventive strategy. *[Article copies available for a fee from The Haworth Document Delivery Service: 1-800-342-9678. E-mail address: getinfo@haworthpressinc.com]*

KEYWORDS. Elder abuse, residential settings, nursing staff, care

INTRODUCTION

Most of the elder abuse research over the last fifteen years has focused on domestic violence (Bennett & Kingston, 1993; McCreadie, 1996; Saveman, 1994); that is, elder abuse within a family context. From Finland, the USA, and Canada, it is estimated that about four percent of the older population (excluding cognitively impaired elderly people) are exposed to abuse (Kivelä, Köngäs-Saviaro, Kesti, Pahkala, & Ijäs, 1992; Pillemer & Finkelhor, 1988; Podneiks, 1992).

Only a few studies deal with elder abuse in institutions or in residential care. They were carried out in a long term care context (nursing homes included) in the USA, Canada, and England and focus on mutual assaults between staff and residents (Pillemer & Moore, 1989), staff being assaulted (Goodridge, Johnston, & Thomson, 1996; Lee-Treweek, 1994) and finally, abuse of residents performed by staff members (Beaulieu, 1992; Lee-Treweek, 1994; Meddaugh, 1993; Pillemer & Bachman-Prehn, 1991; Pillemer & Moore, 1989; 1990). Several authors have conducted literature reviews and made theoretical assumptions about elder abuse in residential care, all of which point to the need for further research (Clough, 1996; Gilleard, 1994; Glendenning, 1996; McCreadie, 1996; McFarland & Hwalek, 1990; Pillemer, 1988; Sengstock, Wierucka, & Goodridge, 1996).

Psychological abuse towards elderly residents seemed to be common among the Canadian and American staffs in nursing homes (Beaulieu, 1992; Pillemer & Moore, 1990). As many as 40 percent of the staff admitted to having been psychologically abusive to a resident and 10 percent acknowledged having carried out at least one physical act towards the patients (Pillemer & Moore, 1989).

There are problems comparing studies because of contextual differences among countries, for example, between the USA and Sweden, with regard to health care organisations, cultural variations concerning tolerance of abuse, and difficulties defining elder abuse in residential settings. Some of the key factors related to residential elder abuse (Pillemer, 1988; Wierucka & Goodridge, 1996) are: (1) the environment of the residential setting which varies between the countries, (2) the staff characteristics, e.g., their educational level, burn out, and staff turnover (cf. Cooper & Mendonca, 1989; Goodridge, Johnston, & Thomson, 1996; Pillemer & Bachman-Prehn, 1991), and (3) the residents' characteristics such as cognitive impairments and communicative difficulties (cf. Coyne, Reichman, & Berbig, 1993; Fulmer & Gurland, 1996; Pillemer & Moore, 1989).

Another difficulty in making comparisons between countries and cultures is the variation in the concepts of elder abuse and mistreatment and their manifestations (see, e.g., Hudson, 1989; Johnson, 1991; Saveman, 1994). Staff may be confused as to whether or not an act in residential care might be abusive. Restrictions on residents is one example: by some people considered as mistreatment but by others as an acceptable act. One way of defining elder abuse in residential care is to present a description of elder abuse such as the one that appears in the European Project Report "Elder abuse/mistreatment in a residential setting means any action or negligence on the part of staff, relatives or relevant other which constitutes inappropriate treatment or which violates the rights of residents and to which the resident objects or could reasonably be expected to object" (Abuse of Older People in Residential Care. A European project, 1997, p. 7). In the present study the term elder abuse is used comprehensively to include physical, psychological, financial, and sexual abuse as well as neglect and mistreatment.

As in other Western countries, the population of old people in Sweden is increasing (Official Statistics of Sweden, 1997). Since 1992, the local authority in the municipalities is responsible for providing social service and care to old people. Elders can either stay in their own homes and receive home care or move into residential settings of various kinds, such as old people's homes, sheltered housings, nursing homes, and group dwellings. All of these residential settings are made as home-like as possible, and the old residents pay a rental fee for living there and for the care given to them. A majority of the elderly people who need this care and service are more than 80 years old, and a large proportion of them have physical and/or mental handicaps or suffer from dementia. There is a particularly close correlation between dementia and old age (Jorm, 1990).

The Swedish research by Grafström and co-workers (1993), Saveman (1994), Saveman and co-workers (1992, 1993, 1996, 1997), and Tornstam (1989) has so far focused on elder abuse in a family context although Tornstam's study (1989) also found that formal carers were reported as abusers of elderly people in their homes. No studies have confirmed situations of elder abuse in Sweden's residential care similar to that reported from other countries. The aim of this study was to investigate the frequencies and types of elder abuse in residential settings as reported by nursing staff in Sweden. One can assume that there are both similarities and differences to other countries, as the contexts vary.

METHOD

A total population based survey was carried out in one area of Umeå, a city in the north of Sweden and in one area of Kalmar, a city in the south. The purpose was to study situations of violence directed against old people living in the residential settings and the staff providing the care and service. Umeå has 103,000 inhabitants, of whom 12,100 are 65 years or older; 1,832 older inhabitants were surveyed. The corresponding numbers for Kalmar are 40,000 inhabitants, of whom 10,200 are 65 years or older; 2,534 older inhabitants were surveyed. The types of residential setting as well as the number of residents and elderly people receiving home care are presented in Table 1.

Respondents

All 640 (320 in each of Umeå and Kalmar) nursing staff, e.g., registered nurses (RN), enrolled nurses (EN), and nursing aides (Na) in non-profit municipal care, with the exception of one private old people's home, were asked to participate in the study. The respondents worked in sheltered housings (old people's homes included), nursing homes, group dwellings, and in elderly people's own homes. Table 2

TABLE 1. Elderly residents per residential setting and number of settings

Residential Setting	Elderly Residents			Residential settings/ home care groups		
	Umeå n	Kalmar n	Total n	Umeå n	Kalmar n	Total n
Ordinary home	70	220	290	1	4	5
Sheltered housing	78	53	131	3	2	5
Group-dwelling	36	78	114	3	4	7
Nursing home	172	84	256	1	1	2
Total	356	435	791	8	11	19

TABLE 2. Total distribution (N) and responses (n) per residential setting

Residential Setting	Umeå			Kalmar			Total		
	N	n	%	N	n	%	N	n	%
Ordinary home	43	39	91	66	52	71	109	91	83
Sheltered housing	30	18	60	55	46	84	85	64	75
Group-dwelling	55	39	71	35	29	83	90	66	76
Nursing home	192	160	83	164	116	71	356	276	78
Total	320	256	80	320	243	76	640	499	78

presents the responses per residential setting, and Table 3, per staff category. In all, 499 (78%) nursing personnel participated in the study, 256 in Umeå and 243 in Kalmar. In Umeå the highest number of respondents (91%) were staff providing care in elderly persons' own homes, while the lowest response rate was found among those working in sheltered housings (60%). The corresponding figures in Kalmar showed the highest response rate among those working in sheltered housings (84%), while the lowest was found among the staff working in nursing homes (71%) (Table 2). Registered nurses in Umeå had the highest response rate (100%), while the response rate among RNs in Kalmar was only 48%. However, nursing aides in Umeå and Kalmar had almost the same response rates (76% and 78%) (Table 3).

The female members of the staff dominated; only seven percent were male. The staff were on average 40 years old (females 41 and males 35 years old) and had worked in their current positions on average seven years. Staff categories, i.e., registered nurses, enrolled nurses, and nursing aids per residential setting are presented in Table 4. Most of the respondents worked day-time and evenings; in Umeå 85% and in Kalmar 62%. In both Umeå and Kalmar about one out of ten respondents worked the night-shift.

Questionnaire

A questionnaire, which included both multiple-choice and open-ended questions about incidences of abuse directed against the staff as

TABLE 3. Total distribution and responses (n) per staff category

Staff category	Umeå			Kalmar			Total		
	N	n	%	N	n	%	N	n	%
Registered nurses	41	39	91	21	10	48	62	51	82
Enrolled nurses	126	99	79	80	62	78	206	161	78
Nursing aides	153	116	76	219	171	78	372	287	77
Total	320	256	80	320	243	76	640	499	78

TABLE 4. Responses per residential setting and staff category (n)

Residential setting	Umeå								Kalmar								Total							
	RN		EN		Na		Total		RN		EN		Na		Total		RN		EN		Na		Total	
	n	%	n	%	n	%	n	%	n	%	n	%	n	%	n	%	n	%	n	%	n	%	n	%
Ordinary home care	0	0	3	3	38	33	41	16	0	0	1	2	52	30	53	22	0	0	4	2	90	31	94	19
Sheltered housing	0	0	9	9	17	15	26	10	0	0	7	11	37	22	44	18	0	0	16	10	54	19	70	14
Group-dwelling	0	0	4	14	17	15	31	12	1	10	11	18	17	10	29	12	1	2	25	16	34	12	60	12
Nursing home	41	100	73	74	44	38	158	62	9	90	43	69	58	34	110	45	50	98	116	72	102	36	268	54
Unknown													7	4	7	3					7	2	7	1
Total	41	100	99	100	116	101	256	100	10	100	100	62	171	100	243	100	51	100	161	100	287	100	499	100

RN = Registered Nurses
EN = Enrolled Nurses
Na = Nursing aides

well as questions regarding elder abuse, was distributed. A description of elder abuse, including a typology of physical, psychological, sexual, and financial abuse as well as neglect and mistreatment was presented in the questionnaire. The questions dealt with background variables, knowledge of elder abuse or own experiences of being abusive towards an elderly resident during the last year, as well as known type and frequency of abuse. The respondents were asked to describe one incidence/situation of abuse of which they were aware. Questions were also included about feelings related to abusive behaviour and prevention of abuse.

Process

Information meetings were held with the staff in all settings before the questionnaires were distributed by the manager at each setting during February 1996. The responses were anonymously collected and sent to the investigators (SÅ) in Umeå and (B-I S) in Kalmar after three weeks. Those who had not returned the questionnaires in time were reminded by a telephone call.

Data Analysis

The data analysis includes frequencies, means, and proportions related to the Umeå and Kalmar groups, to category of staff, and to type of residential setting. In the analysis of the elder abuse questions, the sub-group of respondents from both Kalmar and Umeå, who reported abuse, are combined and treated as one group (n = 55). The internal missing values varied between 4 and 10 percent.

The open-ended answers in the questionnaire were categorised according to their content; for example, type of abuse, solution to the situation, and characteristics of the abuser. The categories of the abuse situations, which are exemplified using quotations in the results, focus mostly on situations involving the staff members. The results from the respondents' own choice of one example of known elder abuse are presented as specific situations. The study was approved by the Ethics Committee of the Medical Faculty, Umeå University and the Faculty of Health Sciences, Linköping University.

RESULTS

Eleven percent (n = 55) of the total respondent group knew of at least one elder abuse incident that occurred during the past year (35 in Umeå and 20 in Kalmar). Most of those who reported elder abuse were nursing aides (n = 24) and enrolled nurses (n = 22). More than two thirds of the staff who reported elder abuse worked in nursing homes (Table 5). Eleven of the staff (2%) admitted that they themselves had used violence during the last year. Ten of them worked in a nursing home and one in a group-dwelling. Seven of them were nursing aides, one was an RN, and three were ENs.

Physical (n = 41, 74%) and psychological abuse (n = 39, 71%) were most frequently reported, followed by neglect and maltreatment (n = 31, 56%). Financial exploitation was reported by approximately 25 percent of the 55 respondents while only one respondent knew of sexual abuse. The abuser was most often reported to be a relative (n = 59) or staff member (n = 40) (Table 6). Nine respondents (16%) reported that they knew of psychological abuse happening daily, and 19 (35%) reported that it happened weekly. Physical abuse was reported to happen at least once per week (n = 12, 22%) and some time per month (n = 14, 26%) (Table 7).

TABLE 5. Reported situations of elder abuse (n = 55) per residential setting and staff category

	Umeå		Kalmar		Total	
Residential Setting	n	%	n	%	n	%
Ordinary home	2	6	5	25	7	13
Sheltered housing	0	0	3	15	3	–
Group-dwelling	3	8	5	25	8	15
Nursing home	30	86	7	35	37	67
Total	35	100	20	100	55	100

	Umeå		Kalmar		Total	
Staff category	n	%	n	%	n	%
Registered nurses	8	23	1	5	9	16
Enrolled nurses	13	37	9	45	22	40
Nursing aides	14	40	10	50	24	44
Total	35	100	20	100	55	100

TABLE 6. Type of abuse distributed per abuser (more than one alternative is possible)

Abuser	Physical abuse n	% of 55	Psychological abuse n	% of 55	Neglect and maltreatment n	% of 55	Financial abuse n	% of 55	Sexual abuse n	% of 55
Relative	16	29	17	31	16	29	10	18	0	0
Staff	14	25	12	22	11	20	2	3.5	1	2
Both	11	20	10	18	4	7	2	3.5	0	0
Total	41	74	39	71	31	56	14	25	1	2

TABLE 7. Type of abuse related to frequency

Frequency	Physical abuse n	Psychological abuse n	Neglect n	Maltreatment n	Financial abuse n	Sexual abuse n	Total n
Daily	0	9	6	1	1	0	17
Sometime/week	12	19	5	1	1	0	38
Sometime/month	14	9	3	2	5	0	33
Sometime/half year	7	2	6	2	4	1	22
Sometime/year	8	5	2	5	3	0	21
Never	14	11	33	46	41	54	169

The Specific Situations that Were Reported

Men were most often the abusers (n = 29, 53%) in the specific situations that were reported. In half of the cases the abusers were relatives (n = 29, 53%) and almost the same number were staff (n = 23, 42%). Distinguishable personal characteristics of the abusers, as mentioned by 37 respondents, were that they were aggressive and easily lost their temper (n = 12, 32%), exhausted and burned out (n = 7, 19%), and/or dominant and egoistic (n = 4, 11%). Mental health problems and lack of knowledge were mentioned as other characteristics.

Two thirds of the abused persons were women (n = 37, 67%). The average age of the abused persons was 81 years; 78 percent were 80 years old or above, the oldest was 96 years old. Most abused persons had more than one handicap/disability (n = 92). They also suffered from dementia disease (n = 38, 41%), mobility disorders (n = 33, 36%), behavioural and/or communicative disorders (n = 10, 11%) and psychiatric diseases (n = 8, 9%). The abusive situation had consequences for the abused old people; fifteen elderly (27%) were said to be more fearful, eleven (20%) became more aggressive, and the same number became confused. Eight persons (15%) reacted with withdrawal. There were also reports of pain, tiredness, and sadness.

The Abusive Situations

More than one type of abuse was reported in the same situation. Physical abuse (n = 44, 80%) was most commonly reported followed by psychological abuse (n = 31, 56%). Eighty percent of the reported abuse occurred in caring situations, i.e., when the elderly persons were helped with their personal hygiene and with activities of daily living (ADL). A few abusive situations occurred in medical treatment situations, such as administration of medication. The respondents described the abusive situations briefly in their own words. The content has been categorized according to whether the staff member was physically, psychological, financially abusive, a combination of these, or circular violence, i.e., when both parties acted/reacted with violent behaviour. Examples of family members as abusers are also given.

Quotations as examples of physical abuse:

> Faeces was removed from a constipated patient in a brutal and degrading way.

> Resident was forced around the corner with great speed.

> One evening when we were seated at the dinner-table one of the staff was in such a hurry when feeding the patient that she did not give the patient time to chew or swallow the food properly. She practically forced the food down his throat. I thought she would suffocate him.

> Care-giver forced care-receiver down on the floor. Held her there and hit her. The care-giver was in a bad mood.

> Cold shower directed into the face.

Quotations as examples of psychological abuse:

> The staff neglect the patient who is often left without supervision and nobody was informed about it.

Noisy care-receiver was told to leave the table and denied coffee. One staff member was mean and sarcastic towards the patient, teased and generally was a nuisance.

Quotations as examples of financial abuse:

The patient was robbed of several thousands by the staff who had withdrawn money on several occasions.

Quotations as examples of a combination of acts:

Rough handling when undressing the care-receiver, swearing, and generally being aggressive towards the care-receiver.

My colleague was helping the patient in the toilet-room when her legs gave way under her. My colleague shouted at the patient and shook her vigorously.

Quotations as examples of circular violence:

The care-giver was fed up and snapped at the patient who shouted back.

A deputy staff member bent the patient's thumb backwards when he tried to hit the care-giver.

The care-giver held the care-receiver and threatened him when he tried to hit the care-giver.

The patient kicked the care-giver, who hit her back in the face.

The demented patient escaped, was aggressive. I grabbed him forcibly.

There were some examples of situations in which the conflict between patient safety and violation of autonomy was marked.

Holding the patient to prevent her from injuring herself and others.

Holding the patient's hand firmly to prevent care-giver being hurt when he was receiving nursing care.

Situations in which a family member was the abuser involved financial matters as well as physical abuse; and the family member was described as rough and violent, when helping the resident with his/her personal care. Quotations as examples of a family member being the abuser:

> Relative giving harsh commands, pulls and tears the old man.

> The husband forcibly pulls the arms and legs of the patient having contractures.

> Relative tends to force-feed the patient.

> The husband pinches the patient, eats her food and kicks her legs.

> The wife is mean to him, throws water in his face when he does not want to take a shower, gives him left-overs, refuses to help him with his medication and is always nagging at him.

> The care-receiver is not allowed to use her own money, e.g., for hair-cuts, foot care or new clothes.

> The wife hits her husband when he does not open his mouth when she helps feed him.

Various ways to find a solution to the problematic situations were described. To talk to the parties involved and to give orders to the abuser to stop the abusive acts were most commonly reported (n = 12, 22%). Another solution mentioned was to have someone step in and divert attention away from the incident towards something else, thereby defusing the situation. Separation of the abuser and the abused person by the staff and visiting restrictions for the abusing relative were also described as solutions to the specific abusive situations. In only one situation was reporting the situation to the police mentioned.

Feelings Experienced Among the Respondents and Coping Strategies

Most of the respondents, who reported elder abuse, said that they experienced a high or moderate degree of powerlessness (n = 41, 75%), inadequacy (n = 33, 60%), outrage at the situation (n = 21, 38%), and shock (n = 18, 33%). A few mentioned a high degree of shame, guilt, loneliness, and lack of knowledge. Specific feelings related to the abuser were described mostly as anger, rage, and disgust (n = 21, 38%), followed by irritation, disappointment, and disassociation. Almost half of the respondents (n = 26, 47%) reported feelings of compassion for the elderly abused persons. More than half of the respondents (n = 30, 55%) mentioned talking about the situation with the team (colleagues) as one important way of handling elder abuse situations. A quarter of the respondents recommended private counselling with the manager.

Preventive Strategies

The most frequently reported preventive strategy concerning elder abuse was more staff education (n = 30, 55%). Almost the same number of respondents suggested staff support to deal with abusive situations (n = 25, 45%). Other possible strategies mentioned were two staff members working together (n = 23, 42%), a test for job suitability at the time of employment, (n = 23, 42%), systematic supervision, more staff (n = 22, 40%) and individual development planning interview (n = 19, 35%).

DISCUSSION

The results from this survey are based on two representative municipalities and can thus be judged to be generalisable to others although the way in which the various Swedish municipalities arrange care for their older inhabitants might differ somewhat. The response rate in this study was high, almost 80 percent, indicating an interest in uncovering the problems of elder abuse. Despite the good response, the violence in specific situations is probably underestimated. Violence within a caring organisation is not in keeping with good quality care and good and proper behavior of the staff. The topic of violence may be taboo; another explanation for underestimation may be that the staff have problems identifying elder abuse (cf. Saveman, Hallberg, & Norberg, 1993). Earlier studies on elder abuse have not reported such high response rates (Clark-Daniels et al., 1989; O'Brien, 1989; Sadler & Kurrle, 1993).

The fact that only 11 percent of the staff reported knowledge of elder abuse is in line with the study of Swedish district nurses, 12 percent of whom reported elder abuse in elderly people's own homes

(Saveman et al., 1993b), and with a random sample of 934 Swedish citizens, 8 percent of whom knew of at least one elder abuse case during the year and 20 percent of those mentioned staff as abusers (Tornstam, 1989). Pillemer and Moore (1989) reported from their telephone interview study of 577 nursing staff in nursing homes that 36 percent had observed physical abuse and 81 percent psychological abuse in the previous year. In the present study only 2 percent of the staff admitted to having been abusive towards an elderly person, while in Pillemer and Moore's (1989) study, as many as 10 percent admitted being physically abusive and 40 percent, psychologically abusive. The difference between the results might be due to research design and cultural variations.

There are problems in comparing the results from the present study with other findings. The organisation of care in Sweden, such as nursing homes and other residential settings, as well as staff levels and work-load, differ from other countries. However, the main findings are in line with those of, for example, Pillemer and co-workers (1989, 1990, 1991). Half of those in the present study who observed abusive situations reported that psychological abuse happened daily or once a week, and one quarter observed physical abuse every week or month. In many situations it is difficult to know whether an act is abusive or not; but when staff members have identified elder abuse, they also tend to report it (cf. Clark-Daniels et al., 1989; Saveman et al., 1993a).

In the present study the staff worked either in residential settings or in old people's own homes. Accordingly, both relatives and staff are potential abusers. However, since most of the reports were from nursing home staff, both relatives and staff may be abusers in residential settings, a situation that has not been addressed in other studies. Three quarters of the respondents knew of other staff members who were abusers. They were reported to be hot-tempered, aggressive, and burned-out. Staff burn-out, residents' aggression, and conflicts are suggested as important predictors of psychological abuse (Pillemer & Bachman-Prehn, 1991).

Most of the reported abuse occurred in the course of nursing activities and mostly involved physically and mentally handicapped old people. Similar results are reported from other studies of elder abuse in a family context (for review see McCreadie, 1996) but have not to our knowledge been reported from studies of residential abuse, which more often seemed to focus on staff characteristics (Pillemer & Moore, 1989; 1990).

The situations described in this study indicate that elder abuse occurs in residential settings. It is possible that the same situation was reported by more than one respondent. The numbers, therefore, cannot be compared directly with other studies, nor should they be used to estimate prevalence. This result indicates the need for more in-depth research in specific cases. However, the situations described are generally in line with other reports (Beaulieu, 1992; Pillemer & Bachman-Prehn, 1991; Pillemer & Moore, 1989, 1990). This study confirms the need of protection for vulnerable elderly people in various residential settings. The consequences for the abused persons, as described in this study, were increased fearfulness and aggression as well as withdrawal. Further studies are needed, where the elderly themselves are the respondents. When Canadian elderly people were interviewed, they reported reacting with sadness and loneliness to many forms of abuse (Beaulieu, 1992).

Feelings of powerlessness and inadequacy commonly reported among the staff in this study were in keeping with what staff have reported when dealing with elder abuse (Dolon & Blakely, 1989; Saveman & Norberg, 1993; Saveman, Norberg, & Hallberg, 1992). They also cited education and support as preventive strategies. In Pillemer and Hudson's (1993) evaluation of a training programme for prevention of abuse in residential settings, the opportunity for the staff to talk openly about the problem of elder abuse, resulted in decline in self-reported abusive actions and reduced conflicts with residents. The educational needs are also highlighted by other authors (Goodridge et al., 1996; Wierucka & Goodridge, 1996).

The main findings indicate that elder abuse involving staff exists in Sweden and is a problem in residential settings as well as in home care. Eleven percent of the total sample were aware of situations of elder abuse. Two percent admitted that they themselves had been abusive towards a resident. Psychological and physical abuse related to caring activities were most commonly reported. In the specific situations reported, the abusers were mostly characterised as hot-tempered, exhausted, and burned-out, and the abused persons were often mentally and/or physically handicapped. A majority of these residents were over 80 years old. The respondents who reported abuse admitted feelings such as powerlessness, anger towards the abuser, and compassion for the abused person. To cope with the situation they talked to each other in the team or to the manager. More education and support were recommended as the primary preventive strategy.

REFERENCES

Beaulieu, M. (1992). Elder abuse: Levels of scientific knowledge in Quebec. *Journal of Elder Abuse & Neglect*, 4(1-2), 135-149.

Bennett, G. & Kingston, P. (1993). *Elder abuse. Concepts, theories and interventions*. London: Chapman and Hall.

Clark-Daniels, C. L., Daniels, R. S., & Baumhover, L. A. (1989). Physicians' and nurses' responses to abuse of the elderly: A comparative study of two surveys in Alabama. *Journal of Elder Abuse & Neglect*, 1, 57-72.

Clough, R. (ed.). (1996). *The abuse of care in residential institutions*. London: Whiting and Birch Ltd.

Cooper, A.. J. & Mendonca, J. D. (1989). A prospective study of patient assault on nursing staff in a psychogeriatric unit. *Canadian Journal of Psychiatry*, 34(5), 399-404.

Coyne, A. C., Reichman, W. E., & Berbig, L. J. (1993). The relationship between dementia and elder abuse. *American Journal of Psychiatry*, 150(4), 643-646.

Dolon, R. & Blakely, B. (1989). Elder abuse and neglect: A study of Adult Protective Service workers in the United States. *Journal of Elder Abuse & Neglect*, 1, 31-49.

The European Commission's PACTE Program. (1997). *Abuse of older people in residential care. A European project*. London: London Borough of Enfield.

Fulmer, T. & Gurland, B. (1996). Restrictions as elder mistreatment: Differences between caregiver and elder perceptions. *Journal of Mental Health and Aging*, 2(2), 89-100.

Gilleard, C. (1994). Physical abuse in homes and hospitals. In: Eastman, M. (Ed.). (1994). *Old age abuse. A new perspective*. London: Age Concern, Chapman and Hall, pp. 93-110.

Glendenning, F. (1996). The mistreatment of elderly people in residential institutions. In: Clough, R. (ed.). (1996). *The abuse of care in residential institutions*. London: Whiting and Birch Ltd, pp. 35-49.

Goodridge, D.M., Johnston, P. & Thomson, M. (1996). Conflict and aggression as stressors in the work environment of nursing assistants: Implications for institutional elder abuse. *Journal of Elder Abuse & Neglect*, 8(1), 49-67.

Grafström, M., Norberg, A. & Winblad, B. (1993). Abuse is in the eye of the beholder. Reports by family members about abuse of demented persons in home care. A total population-based study. *Scandinavian Journal of Social Medicine*, 21, 247-255.

Hudson, M. (1989). Analyses of the concepts of elder mistreatment: Abuse and neglect. *Journal of Elder Abuse & Neglect*, 1, 5-25.

Johnson, T.F. (1991). *Elder mistreatment. Deciding who is at risk*. Westport, Connecticut: Greenwood Press.

Jorm, A.F. (1990). *The epidemiology of Alzheimer's disease and related disorders.* London: Chapman and Hall.

Kivelä, S-L., Köngäs-Saviaro, P., Kesti, E., Pahkala, K., & Ijäs, M-L. (1992). Abuse in old age–Epidemiological data from Finland. *Journal of Elder Abuse & Neglect,* 4(3), 1-18.

Lee-Treweek, G. (1994). Bedroom abuse: The hidden work in a nursing home. *Generations Review,* 4(1), 2-4.

McCredie, C. (1996). *Elder abuse: Update on research.* London: Age Concern, Institute of Gerontology, King's College London.

Meddaugh, D.I. (1993). Covert elder abuse in nursing home. *Journal of Elder Abuse & Neglect,* 5(3), 21-37.

O'Brien, J. (1989). Elder abuse and the physician: Factors impeding recognition and intervention. In Wolf, R.S. & Bergman (eds.), *Stress, conflict and abuse of the elderly.* Jerusalem: JDC-Brookdale Institute of Gerontology and Adult Human Development, pp. 51-60.

Official Statistics of Sweden (1997). *Statistical yearbook of Sweden.* Örebro: Statistics Sweden Publication Service, p. 40.

Pillemer, K. (1988). Maltreatment of patients in nursing homes: Overview and research agenda. *Journal of Health and Social Behavior,* 29 (September), 227-238.

Pillemer, K. & Bachman-Prehn, R. (1991). Helping and hurting. Predictors of maltreatment of patients in nursing homes. *Research on Aging,* 13(1), 74-95.

Pillemer, K. & Finkelhor, D. (1988). The prevalence of elder abuse: A random sample survey. *The Gerontologist,* 28(1), 51-57.

Pillemer, K. & Hudson, B. (1993). A model abuse prevention program for nursing assistants. *The Gerontologist,* 33(1), 128-131.

Pillemer, K. & Moore, D.W. (1989). Abuse of patients in nursing homes: Findings from a survey of staff. *The Gerontologist,* 29(3), 314-320.

Pillemer, K. & Moore, D.W. (1990). Highlights from a study of abuse of patients in nursing homes. *Journal of Elder Abuse & Neglect,* 2(1-2), 5-29.

Podnieks, E. (1992). National survey on abuse of the elderly in Canada. *Journal of Elder Abuse & Neglect,* 4(1-2), 5-58.

Sadler, P.M. & Kurrle, S.E. (1993). Australian service providers' responses to elder abuse. *Journal of Elder Abuse & Neglect,* 5, 57-75.

Saveman, B-I. (1994). *Formal carers in health care and the social services witnessing abuse of the elderly in their homes.* Umeå: Umeå University Medical Dissertations, New Series No 403.

Saveman, B-I. & Hallberg, I.R. (1997). Interventions in hypothetical elder abuse situations suggested by Swedish formal carers. *Journal of Elder Abuse & Neglect,* 8, 1-19.

Saveman, B-I., Hallberg, I.R. & Norberg, A. (1993a). Identifying and defining elder abuse, as seen by witnesses. *Journal of Advanced Nursing,* 18, 1393-1400.

Saveman, B-I., Hallberg, I.R., Norberg, A. & Eriksson, S. (1993b). Patterns of abuse of the elderly in their own homes as reported by district nurses. *Scandinavian Journal of Primary Health Care,* 11, 111-116.

Saveman, B-I., Hallberg, I.R. & Norberg, A. (1996). Narratives by district nurses about elder abuse within families. *Clinical Nursing Research–An International Journal*, 5, 220-236.

Saveman, B-I. & Norberg, A. (1993). Cases of elder abuse, interventions and hopes for the future, as reported by home service personnel. *Scandinavian Journal of Caring Sciences*, 7, 21-28.

Saveman, B-I., Norberg, A. & Hallberg, I.R. (1992). The problems of dealing with abuse and neglect of the elderly: Interviews with district nurses. *Qualitative Health Research*, 2(3), 302-317.

Sengstock, M.C., McFarland, M.R. & Hwalek, M. (1990). Identification of elder abuse in institutional settings: Required changes in existing protocols. *Journal of Elder Abuse & Neglect*, 2(1-2), 31-50.

Tornstam, L. (1989). Abuse of elderly in Denmark and Sweden. Results from a population study. *Journal of Elder Abuse & Neglect*, 1, 35-44.

Wierucka, D. & Goodridge, D. (1996). Vulnerable in a safe place: Institutional elder abuse. *Canadian Journal of Nursing Administration*, 4(3), 82-104.

Enhancing the Quality of Care
in Residential and Nursing Homes:
More than Just a Professional Responsibility

Mike Nolan, RGN, RMN, PhD

SUMMARY. This article highlights a range of issues considered essential to improving the quality of care received by older people in residential and nursing home settings. It is argued that improving such care represents a societal as well as a professional responsibility and that remedial action is needed at a number of levels. Five 'routes' to achieving quality are outlined, and it is suggested that these are not simply alternatives but that each requires attention if genuine progress is to be made. *[Article copies available for a fee from The Haworth Document Delivery Service: 1-800-342-9678. E-mail address: getinfo@haworthpressinc.com]*

KEYWORDS. Older people, residential homes, nursing homes, quality of care

INTRODUCTION

The prevalence of poor, sub-standard, and abusive care in residential and nursing home settings is not known with any precision but is

Mike Nolan is Professor of Gerontological Nursing, University of Sheffield, Department of Gerontological and Continuing Care Nursing, Samuel Fox House, Northern General Hospital, Herries Road, Sheffield S5 7AU, United Kingdom.

[Haworth co-indexing entry note]: "Enhancing the Quality of Care in Residential and Nursing Homes: More than Just a Professional Responsibility." Nolan, Mike. Co-published simultaneously in *Journal of Elder Abuse & Neglect* (The Haworth Maltreatment & Trauma Press, an imprint of The Haworth Press, Inc.) Vol. 10, No. 1/2, 1999, pp. 61-77; and: *Elder Abuse and Neglect in Residential Settings: Different National Backgrounds and Similar Responses* (ed: Frank Glendenning, and Paul Kingston) The Haworth Press, Inc., 1999, pp. 61-77. Single or multiple copies of this article are available for a fee from The Haworth Document Delivery Service [1-800-342-9678, 9:00 a.m. - 5:00 p.m. (EST). E-mail address: getinfo@haworthpressinc.com].

almost certainly underestimated (Glendenning, 1997). The phenomenon is not a new one; and as Victor (1997) notes, reports go back over
30 years to seminal studies such as those of Townsend (1964) and
Robb (1967). Our understanding of what precipitates such poor care,
exactly how it is manifest, and what can be done to prevent it has,
however, evolved little in the intervening period. In a comprehensive
review of the available literature Glendenning (1997) argues that there
is more than a hint of a suggestion that the issue has been glossed over
following many public reports, and indeed, deliberately excluded from
important government statements on institutional care in the UK such
as the Wagner Report (1988). He makes a plea for greater recognition
of abuse in such environments and calls for the investment of research
monies to begin more in-depth empirical study (Glendenning, 1997).
Further study is required, for to date theoretical models to explain or
account for poor care in institutional settings have focused on factors
such as the nature of the care environment and staff/patient characteristics (Pillemer, 1988; Phillipson & Biggs, 1992). There is no doubt
that these are important considerations, but it is a fundamental premise
of this article that attention to such factors alone is unlikely to provide
a satisfactory explanatory framework nor a comprehensive basis for
remedial action. It is suggested here that there are five 'routes' to
achieving quality care and that each needs addressing if the present
situation is to improve. These routes are:

- Making homes a quality option
- Facilitating a quality choice
- Reconceptualising quality outcomes
- Valuing quality staff
- Creating a quality perception

Each of these areas is now considered in turn.

Making Homes a Quality Option

Countries throughout the developed world are currently promoting
a policy of community care in response to the ageing of their populations (Evers, 1995; Davies, 1995). Although the concept of community care is not a new one there has been a shift in emphasis over recent
times towards care by the community, in which the majority of support
needed is provided by family carers in their own or the older persons'

home (Victor, 1997). Victor (1997) cites Meredith (1995) who argues that the ideal of community care is underpinned by four core beliefs, two of which explicitly promote the superiority of home care over institutional care: older people would prefer to live in their own homes and institutions are unable to provide personalised, individualised care and stimulating environments. These taken-for-granted assumptions have been implicitly reinforced by the sustained academic critique of institutional care which has helped foster and perpetuate the negative public perceptions of anything other than living at home. Entry to care is therefore often seen as the 'final sign of failure' (Victor, 1992) and is rarely actively sought by older people. Indeed, in a pan-European review, Jani-le Bris (1993) concludes that 'hostility to residential care is ubiquitous in Europe.' This is a perception that must be countered for two principal reasons:

- Some form of institutional alternative will always be required (Jani-le Bris, 1993; Victor, 1997) and
- the critique of institutional care does not mean that care at home is inherently any better.

As Willcocks (1986) contends, the case against institutional care is incomplete and is based primarily on historical failure rather than a balanced assessment of actual potential. Indeed Lawrence et al. (1987) suggest that it was only during the 1980s that we were 'helped to discover' that living at home was good for us. In a cogent paper Baldwin et al. (1993) detail the sustained attack against institutional care but contend that such critiques have been both unidimensional and unidirectional and are guilty of presenting a static view which projects residents 'devoid of their pasts and denied their futures' (Baldwin et al., 1993, p. 70). Developing their arguments further they contend that there has been a dearth of comparative studies with similarly frail populations in community settings and a consequent uncritical acceptance of the supposed superiority of community care. They pose the question: What quality of life do frail older people really achieve at home? They note:

> Many older people at home cope without the benefit of regular care. In such circumstances depersonalisation, loneliness, withdrawal and depression may be common and might in other contexts be described as institutionalisation. (Baldwin et al., p. 75)

They suggest that there is a need to adopt an open-mind and develop a more informed view that takes into account the interaction between dependence, independence, and interdependence in the care of frail older people in all care settings. This is a point that will be developed further later in this article.

One of the basic challenges, therefore, is the need to counter the currently prevalent perception that institutional care is 'universally dysfunctional' (Higham, 1994). This will require the portrayal of a 'new face' of institutional care so that it is seen as a desirable and accessible option (Salvage, 1995). Without this initial step those who enter care are indeed likely to see this as a 'failure,' those who may have to place them in care (most often family carers) will see themselves as 'failures' and staff who work in such care environments are unlikely to receive the appropriate recognition for the work they undertake.

Facilitating a Quality Choice

The ability to exercise choice, to maintain an element of control, and to see entry to care as being either voluntary and desirable or legitimate, have been known for some time to be critical variables in the process of relocation (Schulz & Brenner, 1977; Rosswurm, 1983; Chenitz, 1983; Willcocks et al.,1987; Porter & Clinton, 1992; Johnson et al., 1994).

Challis and Bartlett (1988) contend that older people should be able to exercise choice on at least four levels:

- When to enter care
- The locality of the home
- Which particular home to choose
- Whether to stay

There is a wealth of research literature to suggest that such criteria are rarely achieved. Some ten years ago it was noted that preparation for entry to care is almost entirely overlooked (Lawrence et al., 1987) and as Booth (1993) contends most people in old people's homes have been put there by somebody else. There is little to suggest that this situation has, or is likely to be, improved.

It is now well established that most admissions to care are made at a time of crisis (Chenitz, 1983; Willcocks et al., 1987; Challis & Bartlett, 1988; Neill, 1989; Sinclair, 1990; Allen et al., 1992; Bland et al., 1992; Reinhardy, 1992; Hunter et al., 1993; Gair & Hartery, 1994; Dellasega & Mastrian, 1995) often following an acute illness and period of hospitalisation. Due to the sudden nature of the admission, older people themselves are often not involved in the decision-making process and are frequently not even consulted (Neill, 1989; Sinclair, 1990; Reinhardy, 1992; Booth, 1993), with the decision either being instigated or made by others, typically family members or professionals, usually doctors (Chenitz, 1983; Willcocks et al., 1987; Challis & Bartlett, 1988; Sinclair, 1990; Bland et al., 1992; Allen et al., 1992; Porter & Clinton, 1992; Gair & Hartery, 1994; Johnson et al., 1994; Dellasega & Mastrian, 1995). Furthermore, despite the putative introduction of consumer choice, older people may enter care without alternatives having been discussed (Roberts et al., 1991; Sinclair, 1990; Allen et al., 1992; Bland et al., 1992; Hunter et al., 1993).

Nolan et al. (1996) suggest that four processes help to determine whether entry to care is a 'positive choice' or a 'fait accompli.' These are:

- Anticipation: the extent to which older people and their carers have planned for admission in a proactive fashion.
- Participation: the degree to which older people and their carers have been actively involved in exercising the choices suggested by Challis and Bartlett (1988).
- Exploration: the degree to which there has been a thorough exploration of: all the alternatives to admission; feelings and reactions to the prospect of admission; the range of possible homes from which to select.
- Information: the degree to which older people and their carers have been given detailed and understandable information on which to base an informed choice.

In considering admission to care in four separate studies, Nolan et al. (1996) concluded that one or more of the above factors were missing in the majority of cases.

The present trend towards ever more rapid hospital discharge (Wistow, 1995) and the emergence once again of the pejorative concept of 'bed blocking' into mainstream professional discourse means that achieving the tenets of a 'positive choice' is likely to prove even more difficult. Indeed as Victor (1997) contends, new funding arrangements in the UK effectively mean that, unless individuals are entirely self-funding, they cannot exercise a choice to enter care but have to meet eligibility criteria set by local authorities. Unless we can begin to address the manner in which people enter care, they may already be fundamentally disadvantaged prior to their move, creating an even more difficult job for those who subsequently have to help meet their needs.

Reconceptualising Quality Outcomes

Given the previously described largely negative perceptions towards institutional care such facilities occupy an increasingly denigrated and ambiguous niche in society. If they are perceived as the environments of 'last resort' (Jani-le Bris, 1993) and are utilised only when other care options have 'failed' (Victor, 1992), what function do they serve and how is it possible to create and sustain quality care? Indeed what does 'quality care' mean in such a context?

One of the fundamental challenges is to conceptualise adequately the care needs of very frail older people. This process is particularly important as levels of frailty and dependence in care environments rise and will continue to do so (Jani-le Bris, 1993; Victor, 1997). Without a basic framework within which to consider key concepts, the quality of life of such individuals cannot be enhanced nor is it possible for an adequate discourse to begin about creating a meaningful and satisfying work environment for the individuals providing care. The unclear or taken for granted manner in which the parameters of good care have been defined effectively inhibits achieving acceptable standards. It is axiomatic that if we cannot define what constitutes 'good care' then its opposite 'abusive care' is similarly vague and nebulous. For example, although benchmarks such as privacy, dignity, independence, choice, rights, and fulfilment (DOH/SSI, 1989) are presented as the hallmarks of good care, what such ideas really mean and how they can be achieved in the context of very high levels of physical and mental frailty is far from clear. Gilloran et al. (1993) argue that it is simplistic and misleading to use 'buzzwords' such as autonomy and individuality without agreement as to their definition.

Moreover, even if consensus as to a definition can be reached, what value do concepts such as autonomy and individuality have for individuals who might be both physically and cognitively frail. To present benchmarks for quality which are either unrealistic, unachievable, or simply inappropriate does nothing to enhance quality of care, and indeed might even hinder it. This is not to argue that such values have no place but rather is a plea for more meaningful discussion about their applicability in all contexts. They are particularly important for staff who, if they set unrealistic or unobtainable goals, are likely to become increasingly disenchanted. For example, one of the basic failures in the nursing care of frail older people has been the lack of agreed outcomes for care. The application of curative or rehabilitative models are often inappropriate (Reed & Bond, 1991) but in the absence of a viable alternative the result is often either 'good geriatric care' in which patients and the ward are kept clean (Reed & Bond, 1991) or 'aimless residual care' (Evers, 1991) where there is no discernible purpose. Such considerations apply equally in all environments which care for frail older people.

In the absence of agreed criteria for positive outcomes it is all too easy for older people to be viewed as commodities. Some years ago Diamond (1986) in the US vividly described the way in which people were treated as 'feeders' rather than individuals who needed assistance to meet their nutritional needs. Eight years later, and across the Atlantic, Lee-Treweek (1994) portrayed a depressingly similar picture of life in a nursing home in the UK. She suggests that the motivation behind the activity of the unqualified care staff, who give the majority of 'hands on care,' is to present the 'lounge standard patient.' This is an individual who is smartly attired and looks neat and tidy whilst on public display in the lounge. Within their work world the presentation of a 'well-ordered body' symbolised a job well done. In order to achieve this it was considered both necessary and legitimate to be ruthless in the delivery of care. Individuals who did not reach the required 'lounge standard' were confined to their own rooms, but in order to ensure that as many individuals as possible were presentable then 'mistreatment and being hard towards patients' became seen as an essential attribute of the good worker (Lee-Treweek, 1994).

It therefore seems of paramount importance that we are able to articulate clearly the aims of institutional care and accord them value and worth in the spectrum of care. Many would argue that maintaining the quality of life of residents is the key purpose (Denham, 1997; Twinning, 1997) but the challenges of identifying what constitutes a good quality of life for frail older people in any setting are well recognised (Stewart & King, 1994; Baltes, 1994; Twinning, 1997). Baltes (1994) suggests that 'ageing well and institutional living' are something of a paradox, hinting that such a statement is perceived as oxymoronic. She argues that there is a need to achieve a delicate balance between overcompensating for deficits by doing too much for older people and optimising potential by placing too many unrealistic demands on older people. This, as Baltes (1994) describes, represents the tension between security and autonomy.

Therefore, concepts such as privacy, dignity, choice, and so on still have an important role to play, as has been reaffirmed in recent studies which confirm their importance in other cultures and contexts (Lowenstein & Brick, 1995), but the challenge becomes how do we achieve these laudable aims at the more extreme ends of frailty where most care is carried out by another individual, and personal space is frequently invaded. It seems clear from most of the recent literature that the key to quality hinges largely on the nature of interpersonal relationships and the recognition that the older person, no matter how frail, has the status of a human being. It is therefore essential that older people are seen to have the potential for continued growth and development, something which is still conspicuous by its absence in many care settings (Koch et al., 1995). Kadner (1994) suggests that intimacy is the essence of a therapeutic interaction and that to achieve this requires the self disclosure of personal information. As Scott (1995) highlights, constructive care requires that staff perceive themselves as an instrument of care and that they have a personal investment in the people they are caring for. In other words caring has no meaning unless the recipient of care in some way "matters." Scott (1995) recognises that this role is a profoundly demanding one in terms of energy, imagination, time, and emotion but as Kayser-Jones (1981) notes 'A personal relationship between staff and the elderly in long-term care institutions is desirable and essential' (p. 49). Developing and nurturing such relationships is not, however, simply a matter of intuition and being a 'good' person, for as Goodwin (1992) points out 'TLC and enthusiasm without proper knowledge and skills is, at best, ineffective and, at worst, disastrous' (Goodwin, 1992, p. 39). This leads to a consideration of the fourth route to quality: the central importance of good staff.

Valuing Quality Staff

Work within institutional environments has never been accorded a particularly high status (Kayser-Jones, 1981; Diamond, 1986; Gilloran et al., 1993; Lee-Treweek, 1994); and in his consideration of the literature on mistreatment and abuse in such environments, Glendenning (1997) draws on the work of Pillemer and Bachman-Prehn (1991) which concludes that well qualified staff do not choose to work in nursing homes. Glendenning (1997) summarises a number of reasons for this: work is physically demanding; financial rewards and status are low; there is a 'high risk' of physical and verbal abuse; and turnover and sickness rates are therefore high which compounds problems of low staffing.

Recent work (Baillon et al., 1996) has suggested that despite positive attitudes towards working with older people, stress levels among staff are high, often due to the lack of support mechanisms and educational opportunities for staff. This was a point reiterated in a recent review of the literature on the importance of training in long-term care environments (Nolan & Keady, 1996).

It has been recognised for some time that the education and training of most professional groups, whether at basic or post qualifying levels, provides an inadequate grounding for work with older people (Redfern, 1988; Kenny, 1988; Gill, 1988), a situation which is compounded by the unidisciplinary nature of most courses. As a consequence many practitioners are poorly prepared for the complexity of needs which older people present. This is particularly so in long-term care settings where, as noted above, the work lacks status and prestige. Nolan and Keady (1996) argue that a number of fundamental prerequisites need addressing before better qualified and trained staff can be recruited and retained in such environments. Therefore, in addition to adequate training in basic skills such as dealing with problem behaviour, wandering and aggression, a range of more therapeutic interventions should be introduced to staff. This provides an important conceptual distinction. For even though there is a need for training in techniques which deal with a particular problem, this alone is too reductionist and is likely to reinforce the perception that older people are basically problematic. To counter this a number of authors have stressed that training for work in long-term care (LTC) must include material on topics such as normal ageing, common pathologies of old age, communication skills, and working with families (Chartock et al., 1988; Weber, 1991; Jones et al., 1992; Kihlgren et al., 1993; Blackmon, 1993; Baltes et al., 1994) before attention is narrowed to particular difficulties. Such training should involve both qualified and unqualified staff and is particularly beneficial when it is multi-disciplinary in nature (Jones et al., 1992; Nolan & Walker, 1993).

As Nolan and Keady (1996) argue however, training must also be linked to a coherent staff development programme, as staff who have been empowered by training need to be exposed to a work environment that values and indeed promotes innovation and change. In its absence the likely consequence is raised but dashed expectations resulting in increased frustration and disenchantment. Training, while important, is a necessary but not a sufficient condition for improved care (Nolan & Keady, 1996). Staff need to have an explicit and agreed philosophy of care (Alfredson & Annerstedt, 1994), with a set of operational parameters derived from that philosophy (Armentorp et al., 1991; Murphy, 1992; Nolan & Walker, 1993). Many advocate the use of an individualised care planning programme for this purpose (Berg et al., 1994; Nystrom & Segerston, 1994).

It is taken as an axiom here that staff cannot provide high quality care unless they themselves feel valued and supported. This is particularly so if they are to develop the close relationships with older people necessary to provide 'constructive' care. Therefore the formation of relationships between staff and individuals in LTC and the provision of stimulating activities must be seen as both a legitimate and a valued activity (Nolan et al., 1995; Lawton et al., 1995), and not viewed as 'skiving' (Gilloran et al., 1995).

Recognising the importance of such 'people work' (Kitwood, 1993) also requires that support for staff is available on at least two levels. First there is a need for positive feedback on performance from peers and managers (Murphy, 1992; Kuremyr et al., 1994; Nystrom & Segerston, 1994; Alfredson & Annerstedt, 1994; Gilloran et al., 1995) in order to reinforce both the competence required to conduct such work and its basic worth. Second there must be explicit recognition of the emotional impact on staff that the forging of close relationships with people in their care engenders (Kuremyr et al., 1994; Scott, 1995; Sumaya-Smith, 1995). Therefore the provision of good emotional support for staff is essential if they are not to exhaust their own emotional resources (Kuremyr et al., 1994), especially when someone dies (Sumaya-Smith, 1995). It has been strongly suggested that the introduction of a system of clinical supervision provides the most effective means of providing such support (Kuremyr et al., 1994; Alfredson & Annerstedt, 1994; Berg et al., 1994).

The above will require continued investment in all staff working in residential and nursing home environments; without this, care is unlikely to improve. The central importance of this was noted over 30 years ago in the Report of the Williams Committee which considered the role of staff recruitment and training in local authority residential establishments in the UK. This concluded with a plea for greater investment in staff, thus:

> Unless this money is spent there is no hope of any significant improvement in the number and quality of the staff who enter and remain in residential work; and unless there is significant improvement in these respects it is not possible to provide the amount and quality of care that is needed. The happiness and welfare of the hundreds of thousands who must be cared for in residential homes depends on our willingness to spend this money. We do not consider the extra cost excessive in relation to the amount of human happiness involved. (Williams, 1967, p. 191-92)

This analysis rings as true now as it did then.

Creating a Quality Perception

Denham (1997) has recently stressed the complex set of issues which need to be addressed before the quality of care in long-term care environments can be improved. This paper has argued that attention to the care environments and staff/patient characteristics, although important, are unlikely to provide a full account or to identify all the areas in which remedial action is needed. Something more fundamental is required. Four 'routes' to quality have been described so far, each operating at a different level of specificity. What is required is a much more proactive response, particularly from the academic and research communities, to create a 'quality perception' of institutional provision so that it is seen as a valued, integral, and essential component of the spectrum of care. Salvage (1995) has termed this a new 'face' for institutional care.

In undertaking some preparatory reading for this Chapter, I chanced across an old news item from the *Nursing Mirror* dating back to January 1983. The headline, written in large letters, read: 'Geriatrics: The Future of Long Term Care.' The report described a workshop about long-term care for elderly people which was attended by nurses, doctors, and social workers 'from all over the country' (the UK). The purpose of the day was to identify some key issues that could form the basis for further discussion and debate, in order to clarify the role and purpose of LTC. In opening the proceedings, the Chairman, Dr. Muir Gray, was quoted as saying: 'It is not so much that we have a system that is going wrong but that we do not have a system.' In reflecting upon this assertion I was struck how, some sixteen years later, it was not only still pertinent but actually increasingly relevant. The intervening period has done little to clarify the role and purpose of LTC but rather has given rise to an even more fragmented, confused, and ambiguous position. Ebrahim et al. (1993) contend that in the UK LTC has been conceptualised almost exclusively in terms of institutional provision, a tendency also apparent in the US (Phillips-Harris & Farnale, 1995), and whilst some authors have provided more encompassing definitions (Kane & Kane, 1991; Kane & Penrod, 1995) there can be little doubt that LTC for most people conjures up an image of often inadequate care provided in bleak institutional settings.

What is required is the adoption of a broader definition of LTC such as that proposed by Kane and Penrod (1995) who define it as 'a wide range of assistance that elderly people with disabilities need to survive and live meaningful lives.' This will include provision in both community and institutional settings so that transition from the former to the latter is not seen as a failure but a natural progression for certain members of the population.

Considerable effort is required in order to raise the profile and status of work with frail older people in residential and nursing homes. Denham (1997) contends that such environments should become part of the training circuit for all medical, nursing, and social care staff working with older people. This goal could be achieved in the UK by further developing the concept of the 'teaching nursing home' (Katz et al., 1995) originally proposed in the US. In moving forward we must identify and promote those environments providing high quality LTC and use them as a training resource. A period of time within such an environment should be an essential component of training for all those who wish to work with older people. This would simultaneously serve both to raise the status of work in LTC and reinforce the important role that such environments play, a role which is in danger of being yet further denigrated in the seemingly remorseless push towards community care (Victor, 1992; Baldwin et al., 1993).

The search for neat and simple causal explorations for the continual failure to improve the care received by the frailest and most vulnerable of our older population is likely to prove fruitless. The issues are complex and inter-related. They extend beyond a professional responsibility and require action at a societal level.

The routes to quality identified here will not provide complete answers and far more empirical and conceptual work is required. Nevertheless, it is hoped that they will prove useful in stimulating the further debate necessary before genuine progress can be achieved.

REFERENCES

Alfredson, B. B. & Annerstedt, L. (1994). Staff attitudes and job satisfaction in the care of demented elderly people: Group living compared to long term care. *Journal of Advanced Nursing*, 20: 964-74.

Allen, I., Hogg, D. & Peace, S. (1992). *Elderly people: Choice, participation and satisfaction*. London: Policy Studies Institute.

Armentorp, N., Gossett, R. D. & Eucherpoe, N. (1991). *Quality assurance for long term care providers*. Newbury Park: Sage Publications.

Baldwin, N., Harris, J. & Kelly, D. (1993). Institutionalisation: Why blame the institution? *Ageing and Society*, 13, 69-81.

Baillon, S., Scothern, G., Neville, P. G. & Bowle, A. (1996). Factors that contribute to stress in care staff in residential homes for the elderly. *International Journal of Geriatric Psychiatry*, 11(3): 219-26.

Baltes, M. M. (1994). Aging well and institutional living: A paradox? In Abeles, R. P., Gift, H. C. & Ory, M. G. (eds.) *Aging and quality of life*, 185-201. New York: Springer.

Baltes, M. M., Neumann, E. M. & Zank, S. (1994). Maintenance and rehabilitation of independence in old age: An intervention programme for staff. *Psychology and Ageing*, 9(2): 179-88.

Berg, A., Hansson, V. W. & Hallberg, I. R. (1994). Nurses' creativity, tedium and burnout during one year clinical supervision and implementation of individuals planned nursing care: Comparison between a ward for severely demented patients and a similar control ward. *Journal of Advanced Nursing*, 20: 742-9.

Blackmon, D. J. (1993). *Nursing assistants in nursing homes: The impact of training on attitudes, knowledge and job satifaction*. Unpublished PhD Thesis, University of Akron, USA.

Bland, R., Bland, R., Cheetham, J., Lapsley, I. & Revellon, S. (1992). *Residential care for elderly people: Their costs and quality*. Edinburgh: HMSO.

Booth, T. (1993). Obstacles to the development of user centred services. In Johnson, J. & Slater, R. (eds.) *Ageing and Later Life*, London: Sage Publications.

Challis, L. & Bartlett, H. (1988). *Old and ill: Private nursing homes for elderly people*. London: Age Concern Institute of Gerontology, Research Paper No. 1, ACE Books.

Chartock, P., Nevin, A. & Rzetlelny, H. (1988). A mental health training programme in nursing homes. *The Gerontologist*, 28(4), 503-7.

Chenitz, W. C. (1983). Entry to a nursing home as status passage: A theory to guide nursing practice. *Geriatric Nursing*, March/April 1983, 92-7.

Davies, B. (1995). The reform of community and long term care of elderly persons: An international perspective. In Scharf, F. & Wenger, G. C. (eds.) *International Perspectives on Community Care for Older People*. Aldershot: Avebury.

Dellasega, C. & Mastrian, K. (1995). The process and consequences of institutionalising an elder. *Western Journal of Nursing Research*, 17(2), 123-40.

Denham, M. J. (1997). Quality issues for older people in continuing care accommodation. In Denham, M. J. (ed.) *Continuing care for older people*, 3-16. London: Stanley Thomas Publishers.

Department of Health/Social Services Inspectorate (1989). *Homes are for living in* London: HMSO.

Diamond, T. (1986). Social policy and everyday life in nursing homes: A critical ethnography. *Social Science and Medicine*, 23(12), 1287-95.

Ebrahim, S., Wallis, C. & Brittis, S. (1993). Long term care for elderly people. *Quality in health care*, 2: 198-203.

Evers, H. K. (1991). Care of the Elderly Sick in the UK. In Redfern, S. J. (ed.) *Nursing elderly people*. Edinburgh: Churchill Livingstone.

Evers, A. (1995). The future of elderly care in Europe: Limits and aspirations. In Scharf, F. and Wenger, G. C. (eds.), *International perspectives on community care for older people*. Aldershot: Avebury.

Gair, G. & Hartery, T. (1994). Old peoples' homes: Residents views. *Baseline* (Journal of the British Association for Services to the Elderly), 54, 24-7.

Gill, P. (1988). *Residential care for elderly people*. Social Work Monographs, Norwich: University of East Anglia.

Gilloran, A. J., McGlew, T., McKee, K., Robertson, A. & Wight, D. (1993). Measuring the quality of care on psychogeriatric wards. *Journal of Advanced Nursing*, 18, 269-75.

Gilloran, A., Robertson, A. & McGlew, T. (1995). Improving work satisfaction amongst nursing staff and quality of care for elderly patients with dementia: Some policy implications. *Ageing and Society*, 15: 375-91.

Glendenning, F. (1997). The Mistreatment and Neglect of Elderly People in Residential Centres: Research Outcomes. In Decalmer, P. & Glendenning, F. (eds.), *The mistreatment of elderly people*, 2nd Edition, 151-62. London: Sage Publications.

Goodwin, S. (1992). Freedom to Care. *Nursing Times*, 88(34), 38-9.

Higham, P. (1994). Individualising residential care for older people. Paper given at British Society of Gerontology Annual Conference, University of London, September 1994.

Hunter, S., Brace, S. & Buckley, G. (1993). The inter-disciplinary assessment of older people at entry into long-term institutional care: Lessons for the new community care arrangements. *Research, Policy and Planning*, 11(1/2), 2-9.

Jani-le Bris, H. (1993). *Family care of dependent older people in the European Community.* Luxembourg: EU Publishers.

Johnson, R. A., Schwiebert, V. B. & Rosenmann, P. A. (1994). Factors influencing nursing home placement decisions. *Clinical Nursing Research*, 3(3), 269-81.

Jones, G. M. M., Ely, S. & Miesen, B. M. L. (1992). The need for an interdisciplinary care curriculum for professionals working with dementia. In Jones, G. M. M., Miesen, B. M. L. (eds.), *Caregiving in Dementia: Research and Applications.* London: Routledge, 437-53.

Kadner, K. (1994). Therapeutic intimacy in nursing. *Journal of Advanced Nursing*, 19(2), 215-18.

Kane, R. L. & Kane, R. A. (1991). Special needs of dependent elderly persons. In Holland, N. W. et al. (eds.), *Oxford Textbook of Public Health Medicine*, 2nd ed. Vol. 3. New York: Oxford University Press.

Kane, R. A. & Penrod, J. D. (1995). *Family Caregiving in an Aging Society: Policy Perspectives.* Thousand Oaks: Sage Publications.

Katz, P. R., Karuza, J. & Counrell, S. R. (1995). Academics and the nursing home. *Clinics in Geriatric Medicine*, 11(3): 503-13.

Kayser-Jones, J. S. (1981/1990). *Old and alone, Care of the aged in the UK and Scotland.* Berkeley: University of California Press.

Kenny, W. T. (1988). Services for the elderly by the year 2000. Education and training issues. *Journal of Advanced Nursing*, 13: 419-21.

Kihlgren, M., Kuremeyr, D. & Norberg, A. (1993). Nurse-patient interaction after training in integrity promoting care in a long term ward: Analysis of video-recorded morning care sessions. *International Journal of Nursing Studies*, 30(i): 1-13.

Kitwood, T. (1993). Person and process in dementia. *International Journal of Geriatric Psychiatry*, 8: 541-5.

Koch, T., Webb, C. & Williams, A. M. (1995). Listening to the voices of older patients: An existential-phenomenological approach to quality assurance. *Journal of Clinical Nursing*, 4, 185-93.

Kuremyr, D., Kihlgren, M. & Norberg, A. (1994). Emotional experience, empathy and burnout among staff caring for patients at a collective living unit and nursing home. *Journal of Advanced Nursing*, 19(4): 670-9.

Lawrence, S., Walker, A. & Willcocks, D. (1987). She's leaving home: Local Authority policy and practice concerning admissions into residential homes for old people, *CESSA Research Report No. 2.* London: Polytechnic of North London.

Lawton, M. P., Moss, M. & Duhamel, L. M. (1995). The quality of life among elderly care receivers. *Journal of Applied Gerontology*, 4(2): 150-71.

Lee-Treweek, G. (1994). Bedroom Abuse: The hidden work in a nursing home. *Generations Review*, 4(2), 2-4.

Lowenstein, A. & Brick, Y. (1995). The differential and congruent roles of qualitative and quantitative methods to evaluate quality of life in residential settings. *Israeli Gerontological Society*, Israel.

Meredith, B. (1995). *The community care handbook.* London: Age Concern.

Murphy, E. (1992). Quality assurance in residential care (Editorial). *International Journal of Geriatric Psychiatry*, 7: 695-7.

Neill, J. (1989). *Assessing people for residential care: A practical guide*. London: National Institute of Social Work Research Unit.

Nolan, M. R. & Walker, G. (1993). The next best thing to my own home: An evaluation of a sheltered tenant housing scheme in Clwyd. Bangor: Base Practice Research Unit, University of Wales.

Nolan, M. R., Keady, J. & Grant, G. (1995). Developing a typology of family care: Implications for nurse and other service providers. *Journal of Advanced Nursing*, 21: 256-65.

Nolan, M. R. & Keady, J. (1996). Training for long term care: The road to better quality. *Reviews in Clinical Gerontology*, 6, 333-42.

Nolan, M. R., Walker, G., Nolan, J., Poland, F., Curran, M., Kent, B. & Williams, S. (1996). Entry to care: Positive choice or fait accompli? Developing a more proactive response to the needs of older people and their carers. *Journal of Advanced Nursing*, 24, 265-74.

Nystrom, A. M. & Segerston, K. M. (1994). On sources of powerlessness in nursing home life. *Journal of Advanced Nursing*, 19(1): 124-33.

Phillips-Harris, C. & Fanale, J. E. (1995). The acute and long term care interface: Integrating a continuum. *Clinics in Geriatric Medicine*, 11(3), 481-96.

Phillipson, C. & Biggs, S. (1992). *Understanding elder abuse: A training manual for helping professionals*. London: Longman.

Pillemer, K. A. (1988). Maltreatment of patients in nursing homes. *Journal of Health and Social Behaviour*, 29(3), 227-38.

Pillemer, K. A. & Bachman-Prehn, R. (1991). Helping and hurting: Prediction of maltreatement of patients in nursing homes. *Research on Aging*, 13(1): 74-95.

Porter, E. J. & Clinton, J. F. (1992). Adjusting to the nursing home. *Western Journal of Nursing Research*, 14(4), 464-81.

Redfern, S. (1988). Services for elderly people by the year 2000. Education and training issues. *Journal of Advanced Nursing*, 13: 418-19.

Reed, J. & Bond, S. (1991). Nurses' assessment of elderly patients in hospital. *International Journal of Nursing Studies*, 28(1), 55-64.

Reinhardy, J. R. (1992). Decisional control in moving into a nursing home: Post-admission adjustment and well-being. *The Gerontologist*, 32(1), 96-103.

Robb, B. (1967). *Sans Everything*. London: Nelson.

Roberts, S., Steele, J. & Morse, N. (1991). *Finding out about residential care: Results of a survey of users*, Working Paper 3. London: Policy Studies Institute.

Rosswurm, M. A. (1983). Relocation and the elderly. *Journal of Gerontological Nursing*, 9(12), 632-7.

Salvage, A. V. (1995). *Who will care? Future propects for family care of older people in the European Union*. Luxembourg: EU Publishers.

Schulz, R. & Brenner, G. (1977). Relation of the aged: A review and theoretical analysis. *Journal of Gerontology*, 32(3), 323-33.

Scott, P. A. (1995). Care, attention and imaginative identification in nursing practice. *Journal of Advanced Nursing*, 21(6), 1196-1200.

Sinclair, I. (1990). Residential Care. In Sinclair, I., Parker, P., Leat, D. & Williams, J.

(eds.), *The kaleidoscope of care: A review of research on welfare provision for elderly people.* London: HMSO.

Stewart, A. L. & King, A. C. (1994). Conceptualising and measuring quality of life in older populations. In Abeles, R. P., Gift, H. C. & Ory, M. G. (eds.), *Aging and Quality of Life.* New York: Springer Publishing.

Sumaya-Smith, I. (1995). Caregiver–resident relationships: surrogate family bonds and surrogate grieving in a skilled facility. *Journal of Advanced Nursing,* 21(3): 447-51.

Townsend, P. (1964). *The last refuge.* London: Routledge and Kegan Paul.

Twinning, C. (1997). Quality of life: Assessment and improvement. In Denham, M. J. (ed.), *Continuing care for older people,* 107-30. London: Stanley Thomas Publishers.

Victor, C. (1992). Do we need institutional care? In Laczko, F. and Victor, C. (eds.), *Social policy and elderly people.* Aldershot: Gower.

Victor, C. R. (1997). *Community care and older people.* Cheltenham: Stanley Thornes Publishers Ltd.

Wagner Committee (1988). *Residential care: A positive choice, report of the Independent Review of Residential Care,* Vol. 1., London: HMSO.

Weber, C. (1991). Training staff to care for people with Alzheimer's Disease. In O'Neill, D. (ed.), *Carers, professionals and Alzheimer's disease, Proceedings of the 5th Alzheimer's Disease International Conference.* London: John Libbey.

Willcocks, D. (1986). Residential care. In Phillipson, C. and Walker, A. (eds.), *Ageing and social policy: A critical assessment.* Aldershot: Gower, 146-62.

Willcocks, D., Peace, S. & Kellaher, L. (1987). *Private lives in public places.* London: Tavistock.

Williams (Chairman) (1967). *Caring for people (The Williams Report).* London: George Allen and Unwin.

Wistow, G. (1995). Aspirations and realities: Community Care at the crossroads. *Health and Social Care in the Community,* 3(4), 227-40.

Potential for the Abuse of Medication for the Elderly in Residential and Nursing Homes in the UK

Ruth Chambers, DM, FRCCP

SUMMARY. Abuse of the medication prescribed to the elderly living in long-stay care homes may be perpetrated by a minority of unscrupulous doctors, pharmacists, or home staff caring for the residents. Disorganised practices and homes, poor communications, and sloppy professional practices may create opportunities for over-dosing, errors, fraud, or theft. This article describes the circumstances leading to the potential abuse of elderly residents' medication, and the measures that may be taken to avoid or minimise such abuse from occurring. *[Article copies available for a fee from The Haworth Document Delivery Service: 1-800-342-9678. E-mail address: getinfo@haworthpressinc.com]*

KEYWORDS. Abuse, elderly, medication, fraud, theft, errors

There has been little acknowledgement of the potential for abuse of the medication prescribed to the elderly residents of registered residential and nursing homes. A small minority of dishonest general practitioners, pharmacists, and/or care home staff may take

---

Ruth Chambers is Professor of Health Commissioning, Primary Care Development Unit, School of Health, Staffordshire University, Blackheath Lane, Stafford ST18 0AD, UK.

[Haworth co-indexing entry note]: "Potential for the Abuse of Medication for the Elderly in Residential and Nursing Homes in the UK." Chambers, Ruth. Co-published simultaneously in *Journal of Elder Abuse & Neglect* (The Haworth Maltreatment & Trauma Press, an imprint of The Haworth Press, Inc.) Vol. 10, No. 1/2, 1999, pp. 79-89; and: *Elder Abuse and Neglect in Residential Settings: Different National Backgrounds and Similar Responses* (ed: Frank Glendenning, and Paul Kingston) The Haworth Press, Inc., 1999, pp. 79-89. Single or multiple copies of this article are available for a fee from The Haworth Document Delivery Service [1-800-342-9678, 9:00 a.m. - 5:00 p.m. (EST). E-mail address: getinfo@haworthpressinc.com].

advantage of old peoples' vulnerable situation for the purpose of financial gain or as a means of obtaining drugs for their own use. A recent review of prescription fraud (Department of Health, 1997) found that the numbers of dishonest practitioners and carers appeared to be low. But there is a low index of suspicion among health professionals who work in a culture of mutual trust. This may mean that fraud goes undetected and the real problem is greater than is realised.

Several key risk factors arise from the ways in which medication is requested, supplied, and distributed to those in residential home care that are conducive to individual elderly residents being purposely deprived of their correct medication or given inappropriate medication. Both of these actions fall into the category of 'elder abuse.' The risk areas concern the procedures that general practitioners and pharmacists use to provide care and medication, inappropriate delegation of tasks throughout the prescribing process without adequate supervision, the lack of monitoring of the quality of care and distribution of drugs to residents, and the laxity of the external inspection system.

The elderly are particularly vulnerable to abuse of their medication being because their evidence may be regarded as unreliable and they may be unable to recollect exactly when and what drugs they took and who provided them. The elderly residents of long-stay care homes often have complicated medication regimes and take several times more medication than those who live independently in the community so that there is more potential for confusion and more to gain from successful fraud or theft.

Staff, working in homes where the internal organisation and management systems are poor, will be likely to make mistakes in the distribution and recording of medication. General practitioners and staff in poorly organised practices are likely to make errors in supplying repeat medication and updating their records. Disorganised homes and practices will provide opportunities for others to commit fraud or steal drugs with little possibility of detection.

The sorts of circumstances where such abuse can arise are discussed below. Examples of such abuse and good practices that might be employed to minimise opportunities for abuse are described.

PROVISION OF PRIMARY CARE
BY GENERAL PRACTITIONERS

Circumstances that May Enable Elderly Residents Medication to Be Abused

The primary medical care provided by general practitioners and their practice staff to the elderly living in long stay care homes in the community has become a political issue. General practitioners resent the expectation that they will take over the medical care of the residents of the vast numbers of residential and nursing homes that have mushroomed over the last decade. There is a debate (General Medical Services, 1997) about whether general practitioners should receive enhanced capitation fees for looking after these elderly residents. Although the National Health Service (NHS) has made financial savings from closing long-stay wards and unblocking acute wards, these funds have not followed the patients. Without paid protected time, most general practitioners are not able to devote the extra time and resources to these elderly residents which their serious medical problems ideally demand. Some doctors have managed to arrange some extra paid time by negotiating payments with individual nursing homes to provide personal services as well as the usual reactive care they provide for any patient on their lists.

Because the workload from a long-stay care home can be onerous, some general practitioners avoid assuming individual responsibility for a care home and divide the medical care of residents in homes among all the general practitioner partners. This lack of a lead general practitioner with responsibility for a home, can reduce continuity of care when inappropriate changes to patients' medication may be overlooked as more than one doctor follows up ill patients.

It has become more common for general practitioners and other doctors to own care homes. General practitioners are required to declare their interests to any prospective residents if they are already patients on their list. Being the owner makes it easier for a dishonest general practitioner or practice staff member to commit fraud by issuing bogus prescriptions or diverting dispensed medication away from the resident or home. If the practice is rural and dispenses medication, the dispensing doctor may be tempted to over-prescribe unnecessary drugs to the elderly just to shift the stock. A dispensing doctor has the power to keep changing medication regimes to increase the frequency of issuing new medication and hence increase the turnover of the stock and consequently the profits of the dispensary business.

General practitioners may have to manage without any medical notes (Graham & Livesley, 1988) for new patients for several months until the notes catch up with the transferred patients. Without notes, the general practitioner has to prescribe repeat medication with unreliable and scanty information about previous medication and medical problems. This can lead to confusion and inappropriate prescribing where fraud or theft of drugs by medical or care staff is relatively easy to commit and difficult to detect.

Homes sometimes have difficulties persuading general practitioners to accept their residents because of the heavy workload compared with that from other elderly patients living independently in the community. Consequently the doctors can dictate the terms and conditions to be fulfilled if they agree to accept residents from the homes as patients. These conditions may include insisting that a home uses a particular pharmacy which is owned by a relative of the general practitioner, for instance, an arrangement where contractor collusion is more likely to occur, resulting in fraud centred on the residents' medication.

Communications between staff in care homes and general practitioners are often poor (Pearson, Challis, & Bowman, 1990). If care home staff call out general practitioners for relatively minor reasons, general practitioners may react by trying to minimise contact with the home whenever possible. The lack of communication may lead to confusion over drugs and recommended changes and provide the background where fraud and theft may go undetected.

Poorly managed practices may issue incorrect quantities or types of drugs. Patient records of medication may be incomplete or out of date. Repeat prescriptions may be inadequately monitored. Such confused systems can allow deliberate fraud or theft by others to happen. Dishonest general practitioners or practice staff might concoct fraudulent prescriptions for individual patients. These may be passed to a colluding pharmacist who does not dispense the prescriptions but claims the fees as if he or she had. Or, false prescriptions may be retained by the fraudster for their own use.

The use of sedatives in the elderly remains widespread despite increasing awareness of the dangers and side effects (Dando, 1997). Inappropriate dosing may be due to inadequate review of the repeat prescription or to enable homes to cope with noisy or aggressive residents regardless of the consequences to the recipients.

Measures by General Practitioners or Staff to Reduce or Deter Abuse of the Elderly Patient's Medication

A practice focus on safe, effective, and rational prescribing makes it difficult for dishonest practitioners and staff to fraudulently withhold or divert drugs. General practitioners should undertake integral monitoring of all stages of their prescribing procedures. This will include regular reviews of the appropriateness of repeat prescriptions (Dando, 1997) and re-assessment of patients' needs and the frequency of re-ordering.

General practitioners should carry current records of medication when visiting individual patients in homes so that they can double check what medication is available. The details in the doctors' notes should be compared with the care home drug charts and any discrepancies resolved. Any changes to medication should be recorded in the care home's drug charts and the patient's medical notes with a fail safe method for transferring details of the changes to the repeat prescribing system back at the practice.

All drugs should be patient-based, rather than stock-based to enable close monitoring that the right drugs are received by the right patients at the right time. If GPs are willing, they should sign the long-stay home's treatment cards to verify residents' medication regimes and make it harder for home staff to divert or withhold prescribed medication. As this is not part of UK doctors' Terms of Service, signing treatment cards will depend on their willingness to co-operate (Royal College of Physicians, 1997).

PHARMACISTS' RELATIONSHIPS WITH NURSING AND RESIDENTIAL CARE HOMES

A dishonest pharmacist working alone or in collusion with the prescribing doctor may substitute a cheaper drug to that prescribed and claim re-imbursement for the more expensive drug dispensed. Colluding contractors may invent drugs for elderly people that are never dispensed but for which fees are claimed.

Pharmacists who want to increase their turnover may set up a service whereby they order repeat prescriptions from the general practitioner on behalf of elderly patients. On the face of it this may be a very helpful service for housebound elderly or hard pressed staff in care homes. But the less patient or carer involvement there is in the prescription request and provision process, the more opportunity there is for fraud or theft of drugs.The system may also lead to over-prescribing if monthly repeats keep being initiated by the ordering pharmacist on behalf of the home for 'as required' medication that is rarely used. There is always the danger that prescriptions intended for irregular use are given routinely when they keep appearing in the drug stock cupboard. An opportunity for fraud occurs if the pharmacist dispenses these 'as required' scripts in full knowledge that they are unwanted and/or recycles the unwanted medication when it is rejected as unnecessary by the nursing home. A pharmacist who is also the owner of the home has more chance of being undetected while committing these sorts of frauds.

Some pharmacists give inducements to homes to retain their business. One example of this might be a drugs trolley given to a home to retain the home's business (Department of Health, 1997). This is a 'grey' area where potential profits for pharmacists gaining dispensing business may be bartered by home owners for their personal gain; in the example given the owner would have had to spend several hundreds of pounds of their own money if the pharmacist had not 'donated' it to the home. This type of arrangement may sully the professional relationship of the serving pharmacist and the home staff rendering further irregularities more likely to occur.

There are several ways in which opportunities for dishonest pharmacists to abuse the medication of elderly residents may be minimised. Community pharmacists should work closely with care homes and the prescribing general practitioners to improve standards of prescribing, drug storage, and administration (Community Services Pharmacists, 1994). So long as it does not conflict with residents' preferences, it is good practice for a home to use the same pharmacist familiar with the residents' usual medication and the home's drug handling and administration systems. But there is a need (Bradley, Taylor, & Blenkinsopp, 1997) for safeguards to limit the risks of collusion and fraud from close working relationships between pharmacists and prescribing general practitioners. Such safeguards include the involvement of patients and carers in the prescription ordering process and the quality monitoring procedures described previously.

Pharmacists should avoid labelling drugs with vague directions, such as 'take as directed' so that there is no confusion about what doses carers should administer (United Kingdom Central Council for Nursing, Midwifery and Health Visiting, 1992). Pharmacists and dispensing doctors should label all medication with typed details of the patient, the name and strength of the medication, the date of dispensing, directions for use, expiration date if appropriate, and any special precautions. If care staff are ever suspected of abusing residents' medication, accurate labelling will mean that such staff would not be able to use illegible writing or alterations as a defence.

QUALITY OF CARE IN RESIDENTIAL AND NURSING HOMES

The person registered as being in charge of a care home must provide 'adequate arrangements for the recording, safe-keeping, handling and disposal of drugs' (Registered Homes Act, 1984) in nursing and residential care homes. Health Authorities interpret the meaning of 'adequate' with different degrees of rigour in their inspection procedures in nursing homes. Social Services have systems in place to make their inspections of residential homes apply more uniform standards. A recent study of the quality of care in 16 nursing homes (Chambers, Knight, & Campbell, 1996) demonstrated that a quality improvement culture was lacking in most of the homes surveyed. Nursing home staff were resistant to audit and monitoring/improving care procedures.

A joint statement by the British Geriatrics Society and the Royal College of General Practitioners (1995) recognised the general lack of investment in training and support of care home staff. Staff working in care homes may be very trusting of other professional colleagues and entirely unaware of the possibility of medication fraud occurring in residential or nursing homes. Agency nurses filling in for regular staff may confuse patients and distribute the wrong drugs to individual patients, if they are unfamiliar with the residents. Agency staff by their very nature of irregular working hours and moving from home to home, might be more likely to withhold individual elderly patients' drugs for their own use.

Much could be done to encourage a quality improvement culture in care homes and tighten controls over the flow of medication into the home and to individual residents. The challenge is to introduce quality systems into homes that minimise the occurrence of errors and reduce opportunities for dishonest activities involving residents' drugs. All care home staff involved in administering medication should be adequately trained to understand the systems, processes, and contraindications to administration.

Repeat medication should be re-ordered in a timely fashion using written or computerised request forms rather than ad hoc verbal messages. Repeat prescriptions should be generated by a doctor, and pharmacists should not dispense medication before a prescription has been issued, except in emergencies when the doctor has given explicit directions to the pharmacist over the telephone and followed this up at the earliest opportunity with a written prescription.

Repeat medication should be ordered by senior members of the permanent residential home staff and records of the orders retained in the home for checking against that received from the pharmacist. The reasons for the absence of any requested items upon collection from the pharmacist should be determined. 'As required' medication should only be reordered if there are insufficient quantities for the patient's anticipated usage in the following 28 day period to avoid stockpiling drugs and to ensure that such drugs are reviewed so that patients are not given them unnecessarily.

The strict regulations about securing all medication in a locked cupboard or trolley should be adhered to (United Kingdom Central Council for Nursing, Midwifery and Health Visiting, 1992). Controlled drugs should be stored in a separate locked cupboard. Keys to all cupboards and trolleys used to store medication must be carried by the person on duty in charge of the home and not left lying around for others to use without permission. Homes need to have careful procedures for disposing of unwanted medication, especially controlled drugs, after their expiration dates, or when residents die or leave the homes.

Drugs should not be left unattended; a maximum of 24 hours of an individual's treatment should be extracted and placed out of secure storage. To avoid mistakes where the wrong patient receives a drug destined for another resident, staff administering medication should check the identity of the resident if they are not regular staff and are unfamiliar with the patient. The label on the medication must tally with that on the drug chart. Staff should countersign the resident's drug chart to confirm which drugs have been given as they do the drug round, rather than catch up on paperwork all at once later in the day. If a drug is discontinued, there should be an obvious annotation in the patient's drug chart. If a drug is changed, it is better for a new prescription to be issued rather than temporary alterations on the pill or medicine bottle. At first sight this may seem wasteful, but it is most important to ensure that inadvertent errors are not made from using altered labelling, and that opportunities for fraud and theft are minimised.

EXTERNAL INSPECTION OF THE QUALITY OF CARE IN RESIDENTIAL AND NURSING HOMES

The more people from outside the home are involved in scrutinising care, the less chance there is for abuse to occur, in this instance, abuse of the medication. Health Authorities employ independent pharmacists to provide appropriate pharmaceutical advice and information in nursing home, but do not necessarily check on the quality of this service. A survey by the Royal College of Nursing in 1994 found that only 64% of homes said that a pharmacist was regularly included in inspections.

The National Association of Health Authorities (NAHA) model guidelines for drugs and medicines for nursing homes (1985) recommend that an authorised pharmacist makes regular inspections to each home at least two times per year. The authorised pharmacist should inspect the methods homes use for storing and recording medicines and that stocks of drugs tally with those recorded as being administered and destroyed. The pharmacist has the authority to question patients about the drugs they have received and the dispensing pharmacists about the drugs they have supplied.

Different Health Authorities have varying standards of inspection of homes that include inspecting the policy management, workload, resources, and service standards in individual homes. It is common for inspections to reveal breaches in the law. One study (Redmayne, 1995) of inspections in 200 residential care homes found inaccurate medication records, sloppy medication procedures, and insecure storage of drugs, in one tenth of homes. A United Kingdom Central Council (UKCC) report (1994) also identified inadequate systems of drug administration, ineffective management, lack of care planning, poor record keeping, and almost non-existent induction and in-service training. The UKCC has actively promoted improved procedures for the management of medication in care homes and has produced a booklet: *Standards for the Administration of Medicines* (1992) that is widely used by all those working to maintain and monitor quality of care in long-stay homes.

There are a great many ways in which the elderly residents of residential care and nursing homes are vulnerable to the abuse of their medication. In cases of fraud, the elderly may be the unwitting tools of dishonest practitioners or carers, and their identities used for bogus prescribing. They may suffer if drugs intended for them are replaced by cheaper alternatives unbeknownst to the prescribing doctor or if their drugs are withheld by unscrupulous thieves. Staff working in disorganised practices and homes can easily make mistakes in prescribing or giving out medication, and dishonesty may be masked by the disorganisation. The elderly are vulnerable and it behoves all medical and care staff to do their best to promote effective and rational prescribing with integral monitoring of the quality of all stages in the prescribing process.

REFERENCES

Bradley, C., Taylor, R.T., & Blenkinsopp, A. (1997). Developing prescribing in primary care. *British Medical Journal*, 314, 744-7.

British Geriatrics Society & The Royal College of General Practitioners (1995). *Joint statement on the care of the frail elderly.*

Chambers, R., Knight, F., & Campbell, I. (1996). A pilot study of the introduction of audit into nursing homes. *Age and Ageing*, 25, 465-9.

Community Services Pharmacists (1994). *Guidelines for the registration and inspection of private nursing homes in England and Wales.*

Dando, P. (1997). Nursing Home. *The Journal of the Medical Defence Union*, 13(1), 22.

Department of Health (1997). *Prescription fraud: An efficiency scrutiny.* Department of Health.

General Medical Services (1997). News report. *British Medical Journal*, 314: 684.

Graham, H.J. & Livesley, B. (1988). Newly registered elderly patients: Who are they and why such delay in the transfer of their medical records? *British Medical Journal*, 296, 340-2.

National Association of Health Authorities and Trusts (NAHAT) (1985). *Registration and inspection of nursing homes: A handbook for health authorities.*

Pearson, J., Challis, L., & Bowman, C.E. (1990). Problems of care in a private nursing home. *British Medical Journal*, 301, 371-2.

Redmayne, S. (1995). *Spotlight on homes for the elderly: An analysis of inspection reports on residential care homes.* Bath Social Policy Papers No 22: University of Bath *Registered Homes Act* (1984). London: HMSO.

Royal College of Physicians of London (1997). Medication for older people. *Royal College of Physicians.* London: Royal College of Physicians.

Royal College of Nursing (1994). *An inspector calls? The regulation of private nursing homes and hospitals.* London: RCN.

United Kingdom Central Council for Nursing, Midwifery and Health Visiting (1992). *Standards for the administration of medicines.* London: UKCC.

United Kingdom Central Council for Nursing, Midwifery and Health Visiting (1994). *Professional conduct–an occasional report on standards of nursing in nursing homes.* London: UKCC.

Neglect and Abuse Associated with Undernutrition in Long-Term Care in North America: Causes and Solutions

Susan J. Aziz, MA
Irene Campbell-Taylor, PhD

SUMMARY. Protein-calorie undernutrition in institutional long-term care is a significant cause of morbidity, mortality, increased health care costs, and poor quality of life. Failure to provide adequate nutrition constitutes neglect, and certain practices associated with feeding the dependent elder or adult with developmental disabilities can be abusive. The causes are multifactorial. They are related to conditions common to these persons; multiple medication use, difficulty in swallowing, gastrointestinal dysfunction, poor oral health and oral care, sensory changes with aging, and lack of education and training in the proper protocols required to provide adequate food and liquid to persons with cognitive and physical impairments. Solutions which are simple, cost-effective, easy to apply and cross national, ethnic, and cultural boundaries are described. *[Article copies available for a fee from The Haworth Document Delivery Service: 1-800-342-9678. E-mail address: getinfo@haworthpress-inc.com]*

KEYWORDS. Swallowing difficulties, medications, oral health, cultural preferences, education, training

---

Susan J. Aziz is Vice-President, Advocacy and Education Programs, WISE Senior Services, 1527 Fourth Street, Santa Monica, CA 90401.

Irene Campbell-Taylor is Clinical Neuroscientist, Research Consultant, Human Neurochemistry, Neurobiology, Neuropathology Laboratory, The Clarke Institute, Toronto, Ontario, Canada (E-mail: IreneCampbellTaylor@medscape.com).

[Haworth co-indexing entry note]: "Neglect and Abuse Associated with Undernutrition in Long-Term Care in North America: Causes and Solutions." Aziz, Susan J., and Irene Campbell-Taylor. Co-published simultaneously in *Journal of Elder Abuse & Neglect* (The Haworth Maltreatment & Trauma Press, an imprint of The Haworth Press, Inc.) Vol. 10, No. 1/2, 1999, pp. 91-117; and: *Elder Abuse and Neglect in Residential Settings: Different National Backgrounds and Similar Responses* (ed: Frank Glendenning, and Paul Kingston) The Haworth Press, Inc., 1999, pp. 91-117. Single or multiple copies of this article are available for a fee from The Haworth Document Delivery Service [1-800-342-9678, 9:00 a.m. - 5:00 p.m. (EST). E-mail address: getinfo@haworthpressinc.com].

o provide adequate nutrition in hospitals, nursing homes
ices for adults with developmental disabilities (DD) has
ified as neglect. This failure can result from, as well as
istances of abuse. Residents in long-term care are, by definition, chronically ill and/or permanently disabled. Conditions common to older adults and to persons with DD frequently have swallowing dysfunction as a prominent symptom (Zahler et al., 1993). These
conditions include strokes, dementias, movement disorders, endocrine
impairment, and gastrointestinal dysfunction (Caruso, 1997; Hilde-
brand et al., 1997; Wang et al., 1997). In addition, a critically important variable is side effects of neuroleptic, psychotropic, and prokinetic drugs (Aman, 1990; Hayoshi et al., 1997; Campbell-Taylor, 1996).

Prevalence rates for malnutrition in the institutionalized elderly
range from 20-60% of patients in hospitals and up to 85% in nursing
homes (Manson & Shea, 1991; Lipschitz, 1991; Coats et al., 1991;
Nelson et al., 1993; Swagerty, 1995). Protein-calorie malnutrition reduces the resident's ability to combat infections and leads to a significant increase in costs related to the use of antibiotics, extra nursing
time, acute care hospital admissions, and plastic surgery for bedsores
(Frantz et al., 1991; Disbrow & Dowling, 1991; Bernardi & McGovern, 1993; ADA, 1993). Provision of food and liquid in long-term care
is usually described as "assistance in eating." It can be much more
than that. The dependent resident must be fed by someone. Feeding is
a task that extends beyond mere "assistance" and requires specific
knowledge and skills.

While it is axiomatic that someone who has difficulty swallowing
will ingest less food, the reasons for malnutrition are multifactorial.
The major source of possible abuse or neglect lies in the fact that the
dependent patient must be fed by someone else. If the feeder has no
understanding of the nature of the problem or believes that feeding
someone else is simple, the scene is set for unintentional psychological and/or physical harm, and/or for feeding little or no food. Feeding
dependent, older persons has been identified as one of the tasks that
nursing staff dislike the most. We suggest that this aversion, stemming
from a lack of knowledge and training and the provision of inappropriate food and liquids, form a basis for possible patient mistreatment,
such as force feeding, feeding too quickly, or not feeding when required.

The fiscal constraints associated with the health care reform movements in Canada and the United States have resulted in an increased use of lower-paid, untrained, unlicensed nursing assistants in long-term care settings. Pillemer and Moore (1989) have speculated that nursing assistants have the greatest opportunity to engage in abusive acts because of their direct and on going contact with residents. A major outcome of their study of elder abuse and neglect in nursing homes (1990) was the design of an innovative training program on the interpersonal aspects of patient care to help nursing staff handle burn-out, stress, and conflict. This program complements training in the technical aspects of care.

In another study of elder abuse and neglect in nursing homes, Paton and her colleagues (1994) found that 11% of complaints received by the Long-Term Care Ombudsman Program dealt with food and nutrition. These complaints were documented separately from complaints relating to resident care, which included elder abuse and neglect, and represented 28% of complaints received.

The Nursing Home Reform Act, enacted by Congress in 1987, developed new standards for quality of care and requires training for nursing assistants on the provision of nutritional care. At the October 1997 Forum on The Risk of Malnutrition in Nursing Homes, held before the Special Committee on Aging of the United States Senate, Kayser-Jones stated that this training does not adequately prepare certified nursing assistants to feed residents safely (US Senate, 1997). At the request of the Senate's Special Committee on Aging, the Government Accounting Office (GAO) conducted a federal investigation into allegations of resident deaths in California nursing homes in 1993 as a result of malnutrition, dehydration, and other serious conditions for which they did not receive acceptable care. The report (US GAO, 1998) concluded that despite the federal and state oversight infrastructure currently in place, unacceptable care was a problem in many homes.

FACTORS CONTRIBUTING TO MALNUTRITION

Swallowing Impairment and Its Causes

We will use the term "swallowing impairment" rather than the more frequently used "dysphagia" in order to avoid ambiguity. Dysphagia, to most physicians, means difficulty in passing food and liquid through the esophagus. While that is an important part of many of the conditions we will describe, the residents discussed here also have significant impairment of the lips, tongue, and throat (pharyngeal muscles) which contribute to the difficulty of ingesting sufficient food and liquid. Also, it should be kept in mind that dysphagia is a symptom, not a disease. The following is a description of only the most common swallowing disorders in older adults and persons with DD.

Strokes

Strokes account for only approximately 3-5% of all persistent swallowing problems. Impairment of swallowing in persons with right-sided paralysis tends to improve spontaneously and relatively quickly (Buchholz, 1994; dePippo et al., 1994; Smithard et al., 1996). In those with right hemisphere damage and left-sided paralysis, the dysfunction tends to be long-lasting and is compounded by a condition known as left neglect or hemi-inattention. In this common but poorly understood phenomenon, the affected persons can see objects on the left, but behave as though the objects do not exist. These residents will shave only the right side of the face, dress only the right half of the body, and ignore anything on the left, including the contents on the left side of the food tray. They are generally regarded by nursing staff as among the most difficult residents, largely because nurses are typically not trained to recognize their unique and unusual deficits. A typical scenario during mealtimes is that the resident, having eaten only half of the contents of the plate or tray, either complains of being hungry or is in some way reprimanded for not eating all of the meal, with predictable results. The misunderstandings that ensue can be, at best, unpleasant and, at worst, abusive. The solution to this problem is to observe the resident during meals, and turn the tray around when the right half of its contents has been consumed. If one examines the set-up of most food trays, the majority of the food is on the left with liquids on the right. Turning the tray and rearranging the food can be done by a volunteer if nursing staff are too few in number to feed residents as well as supervise those who need only occasional assistance.

Movement Disorders

Parkinson's disease (PD), amyotrophic lateral sclerosis (ALS), Huntington disease (HD), multiple sclerosis (MS), cerebral palsy (CP) with impairment of oral muscle activity, and many inherited disorders have swallowing impairments (Lamprecht, 1990; Leopold, 1996). The most significant difficulty occurs within the mouth itself, followed by dysfunction of the pharyngeal muscles and gastroesophageal reflux (ascent of stomach contents into the esophagus) that often directly affects the oral and pharyngeal stages of swallowing (Quigley, 1996; Nilsson et al., 1996; Leopold & Kagel, 1997). In addition, many have associated gastrointestinal problems that affect the ability to pass food into the stomach and slow normal stomach emptying. This phenomenon can have particularly serious consequences as will be described later.

The inability to hold, chew, and manipulate a mouthful of food and prepare it for swallowing leads to overall poor control in both mouth and pharynx. The major way in which the mouth is cleaned after eating is by moving the tongue around to dislodge pieces of food and to make sure that no particles are left in the oral cavity. Observation of residents with swallowing dysfunction will show that they rarely, if ever, perform these movements. Discoordination of the muscles in the throat necessary to propel the food toward the opening to the esophagus usually causes misdirection toward the airway with coughing, choking, and, often, inhalation (aspiration) of the food or liquid. At worst, it causes blockage of the airway with fatal results.

Many of the diseases mentioned above have, as part of the disease itself, an associated impairment of the esophagus and stomach. This is particularly true of PD and is of major significance in the delivery of anti-Parkinsonian medication (Poewe, Lees, & Stern, 1988; Edison et al., 1996). Levodopa-carbidopa must reach the duodenum, past the stomach, as quickly as possible. If it does not, it cannot enter the brain and, therefore, has no effect. Gastroparesis, or slow stomach emptying, is part of PD, so that medication frequently does not reach the duodenum quickly enough. Residents may develop a worsening of symptoms, not because the disease is progressing, but because the medication is ineffective. Swallowing becomes even more difficult, and special consistency foods with specific feeding techniques are essential.

Medications are frequently given when the resident is already in bed or about to lie down. In healthy young adults, it has been shown that, if consumed in this fashion, pills may stay in the esophagus for hours. A situation recognized by many nurses is that of the elderly resident who is given night-time sedation in this fashion and in whom it does not take effect for several hours. It is then believed that the dosage is too low, and the medication is increased, leading to severe lethargy in the morning. If the medication were to be given properly, with the resident upright for at least an hour before lying down, possible overdosing is avoided.

Pills can also become stuck in the throat or the esophagus. Any medication that remains in the esophagus will be ineffective unless it can be absorbed through the skin (Channer & Virjee, 1986). Some caustic drugs can burn the esophagus, resulting in ulceration. Failure to consider these aspects of medication delivery can cause significant pain. More importantly, this practice can delay or inhibit the effects of the medication, leading to false assumptions about necessary dosage and efficacy. The physician who, typically, on weekly or monthly visits, may not even see the resident, is advised by nursing staff that a certain medication is "not working" and may increase the dosage or change the medication.

Gastroesophageal Disorders

Disorders of the stomach and esophagus are caused not only by disease processes, e.g., diabetes, and congenital impairments, but by aging itself (Sundkvist et al., 1991; Aviv, 1994; Robbins et al., 1995). In this, we must include many persons with DD, who tend to age faster physiologically than chronologically. The outstanding example is Down's syndrome, victims of which must be considered middle-aged in the late third decade, even though many are surviving to advanced ages because of better medical care during infancy and childhood.

An elderly diabetic patient has difficulty in passing food through the esophagus and takes several times the normal length of time to empty the stomach (gastroparesis diabeticorum) (Bergstrom, 1988; Nompleggi et al., 1989; Lamey et al., 1992). Gastroesophageal reflux (GER) is also common in older adults and in persons with DD. Estimates range as high as 75% (Parkman & Fisher, 1997). This phenomenon has several effects. GER can directly affect the coordination of the muscles of swallowing (Richter et al., 1987). Stomach acid, if it rises back up the esophagus, can come in contact with receptors just above the entrance to the stomach that, by a complex feedback system, affects the swallow and/or the lungs. We now know that a significant number of adults with asthma actually have nighttime reflux, causing waking with wheezing, coughing, and gasping (Feinberg & Tully, 1989; Feinberg et al., 1990; Ayers & Miles, 1996; Woo & Ross, 1996). The deepest part of sleep is the usual time for reflux to occur, as this is the period during which all muscles relax and swallowing of saliva stops. Because it usually occurs during the night or with no visible sign, aspiration of reflux is commonly missed as a cause of swallowing dysfunction and pneumonia. All vulnerable residents, i.e., the majority of the chronically ill elderly and persons with DD, should sleep with the bed placed in a position with the head higher than the feet by approximately 20 to 30 degrees and the mattress straight (Reverse Trendelenberg position) and treated at all times with the nursing protocol known as "anti-reflux regime," avoiding any pressure on the stomach.

With GER, the swallow can become discoordinate, with frequent coughing and choking, or the resident may complain of food, particularly bread and meat, sticking in the throat when it is actually stuck in the esophagus (Parkman & Fisher, 1997; Triafilopoulos et al., 1992; Boeck et al., 1997). Fear of eating can become overwhelming. Gastroparesis can be mistaken for anorexia or for refusal to eat. It is common for both elders and persons with DD to eat well at breakfast, eat little at lunch and then have a small supper. It is rarely recognized that they are simply not hungry because the stomach is still full. It is only after the long overnight fast that hunger appears and a sufficient breakfast is eaten. The cycle then begins all over again. Demented or otherwise non-communicative residents frequently experience hunger close to bedtime, when the stomach has had a chance to empty. They may act aggressively, or wander, being unable to express the reason for their discomfort. This can be mistaken for aberrant behavior ("sundowning") caused by confusion or dementia. Sedation is given, and the patient is put to bed. As a cost-saving measure, many nursing homes use a high percentage of fats as a source of energy in the foods supplied. Fat slows gastric emptying, thus compounding the problem.

Medications

The issue of polypharmacy in both older adults and persons with DD is well documented (Ouslander, 1981). Many, if not most, of the medications commonly prescribed have, as a universal side effect, dry mouth (xerostomia). When the mouth is dry, the swallow becomes discoordinate, even when swallowing liquid, the most difficult consistency to swallow without choking. Older adults do not produce as much saliva as younger adults do, and their saliva tends to be thicker (Rhodus, 1990; Vissink et al., 1996). Saliva is essential to clean the mouth, start the process of digestion when mixed with food, lubricate the food enabling smoother passage toward the esophagus, and neutralize small amounts of refluxed stomach acid, thus protecting the lining of the esophagus and reducing the effects of reflux on the swallow. In elderly females, a condition known as Sjogren's syndrome, or sicca syndrome, has, as prominent features, dry mouth and dry eyes. This is an autoimmune disorder that is significantly underdiagnosed in elderly females and has a very high rate of associated swallowing and esophageal disorders (Zou, Zhang, & Hua, 1995; Sciobba, 1994; Anselmino et al., 1997; AHCPR, 1991).

Another, serious and potentially life threatening side effect of drugs that affect the central nervous system is tardive dyskinesia (TD). TD is easily identified and results solely from long-term (or sometimes short-term) use of medications such as haloperidol, risperidone, and phenothiazines (Casey & Rabius, 1978). TD presents as repetitive lip smacking and chewing movements. It disrupts the ability to control the food within the mouth and to swallow safely. It is associated with a high incidence of choking. Deaths from choking in psychiatric hospitals are 100 times that of the general population and are believed to be associated with the medications used (Hayashi et al., 1997).

Changes in Taste and Smell

The thresholds of taste sensation rise as one ages so that it takes a greater concentration of a given taste to produce the same sensation. The exception is the sense of sweet (Cain, Reid, & Stevens, 1990). Most nurses notice that elderly persons prefer sweet foods, often eating dessert only, and they tend to interpret this as a willful refusal to eat the "nourishing" food. In a sense, this attitude is the product of many cultures' insistence that children eat all the spinach before getting the sweet. There is also evidence that babies prefer sweet tastes, and this may be an adaptive mechanism. It is rare to find a poisonous food that is also sweet, so that early humans, when foraging for food, were to some degree protected by a preference for sweet and an aversion to bitter tastes. Taste sensation can also be altered by many of the drugs commonly prescribed for long-term care residents (Myer, Hartmann, & Kuhn, 1996). The sense of smell diminishes with age, is affected by certain drugs, and is one of the earliest symptoms of PD and, although this is not quite so well established, of Alzheimer's disease (Stevens et al., 1995; Wenning et al., 1995; Yagamishi, Takam, & Getchell, 1995; Priefer & Robbins, 1997). Taste depends on an intact sense of smell (Poothulli, 1995; Huttenbrink, 1995). Without adequate olfaction, food is tasteless and appetite reduced. Foods for institutional meals are commonly chosen by food service supervisors or dietitians who tend to be young adults. The foods they choose do not taste the same to the residents who are required to eat them.

Lack of Attention to Cultural Food Preferences

Individual food preferences can also relate to an elder's cultural, racial, or religious background. In her study of nursing home residents who were not eating well, Kayser-Jones found that for the most part, Western food was served to everyone, despite the fact that 33% of the residents were members of minority groups. Lack of attention to individual food preferences was one of the most predominant factors that influenced the nutritional intake of residents (USGAO, 1998). A Chinese resident lost 31 pounds, or 30% of his body weight, over a six-week period. His weight fell from 102 to 71 pounds at the time of his death.

Poor Oral Health and Oral Care

The process of aging produces causes changes in sensation in the mouth and throat (Dolan et al., 1990). This causes a predisposition to choking on misdirected food and liquid. The lungs become less resilient, cough reflexes diminish, and the ability to protect the airway and clear the lungs by coughing is reduced. The majority of healthy individuals aspirate saliva during the deepest part of sleep. If the mouth contains gum disease, tooth decay, or plaque, the aspirated saliva carries bacteria into the lungs (Loesche, 1991; Lenander-Lumikari & Johansson, 1995; Hirota et al., 1997). Poor or inconsistent oral care contributes not only to poor appetite but also to the development of nosocomial, or "nursing home," pneumonia (Sciubba, 1996; Lynch, 1994). Malnutrition and its accompanying immune suppression frequently allows the development of fungi in the mouth (oral candidiasis or "thrush") that is extremely uncomfortable and can contribute to the development of fungal pneumonia as well as further diminishing appetite. This is caused by the same organism as athlete's foot. It does not take a great deal of imagination to realize how disturbing it would be to have the same burning sensation in the mouth and throat. As a matter of nursing routine, consistent oral care is rarely given, particularly to residents who are edentulous. These individuals require oral care on a regular basis, if only to remove food debris that tends to remain in the mouth because of poor tongue mobility. The resident who "pockets" food is presumed to be refusing to swallow. In fact, this common occurrence is caused by poor ability to manipulate the food within the mouth and move it backward in preparation for swallowing. There is a simple technique that overcomes this problem, but again, there is a general lack of understanding of the problem and of the techniques of feeding that can solve it.

Residents who wear dentures are noted to use them less, decreasing the ability to chew. One of the reasons that dentures fail to fit is that they are allowed to sit in air and dry out. If they are made of acrylic material, this drying alters the shape so that they no longer fit when replaced in the mouth. In addition, the use of denture adhesives can reduce swallowing ability, as many contain substances that are anesthetizing. For dentures, particularly the upper, good fit depends on the suction created by a combination of saliva and mucus within the oral cavity. If a resident has a dry mouth, as most do, the fit of dental prostheses is problematic. Care of a dependent resident's dentures is a nursing task and one that is all too often neglected (Niedermeier & Kramer, 1992; Ship et al., 1996; Hirota et al., 1997).

Financial Considerations

Cost Containment

It is generally agreed that the amount of money per resident, per day typically allotted to nursing homes is insufficient. In an attempt to contain costs as well as in the conviction that it is more appropriate for residents with swallowing problems or who lack teeth, many institutions blenderize their foods into a thin puree. In most cases this leads to undernutrition. A constant diet of puree diminishes whatever swallowing ability remains. Also, to blenderize food, liquid is added, thereby increasing the volume per serving. This is usually too much for the resident to consume. In addition, nursing staff tend to serve what they perceive to be a "normal" serving, not realizing that the entire dish must be eaten for proper nutrition. Food of a mousse or pudding-like consistency is best, for reasons to be discussed later.

Food Waste

Failure to provide food of appropriate consistency and flavor leads to a significant amount of waste, with millions of dollars per annum being literally thrown away (Intintoli & Woulfin, 1990). The preparation of suitable consistency, nutrient-dense food would not only improve the residents' nutritional status but save a considerable amount of health care dollars. There are many commercial producers of suitable, appetizing foods. Unfortunately, the cost per serving is often perceived to be too expensive. The administrators and dietitians responsible for purchasing are unaware of the extent of food waste and its effect on costs and resident well-being.

Lack of Education and Training in the Proper Protocols

Oral Feeding

Very few schools of nursing teach the proper techniques for feeding a dysphagic patient. The task of feeding is usually given to the least trained staff members. There is a lack of awareness that feeding the swallowing-impaired patient is a skilled nursing task, requiring special training and having its own protocol (Siebens et al., 1986; Sanders, 1990; Hall, 1994; Hansel & Heinemann, 1996; Helzopfel et al., 1996). It must be kept in mind that, simply because it is a skilled task does not mean that persons other than nurses cannot learn the required skills. Giving injections is a nursing task, but even children with diabetes learn to perform their own injections several times a day.

The first common error in feeding is having a patient either in bed or in a chair, being fed by someone standing over them. This requires that the patient raise the chin, thus opening the airway and increasing the risk of misdirection of the bolus. One has only to think of taking a mouthful of water, looking up at the ceiling and trying to swallow. There is an immediate awareness that this is not a natural position and that there is a danger of choking. The second is failure to teach proper spoon-feeding techniques. The third is that of feeding too quickly, leading to more choking and general anxiety in both the patient and the nurse. The reason given for this situation is usually a shortage of staff and time. If it is realized that feeding is a critically important skilled nursing task, that reason becomes as untenable as saying that there is not enough time to change dressings in the prescribed fashion, or taking blood pressures carefully and accurately.

The rate of feeding is extremely important. Everyone swallows twice per mouthful; once to ingest the major part of the bolus, followed by a "clearing" swallow. If healthy individuals do this, then the swallowing impaired patient requires even more time in which to clear the mouth for the next swallow. Near-fatal choking episodes have been reported in patients who were on "dysphagia," i.e., consistency adjusted, diets. The choking related directly to being fed too quickly. Not having enough staff or time in which to feed patients is, at least in part, a misperception, as there are ways in which to accommodate to this real problem that are of advantage to both staff and patients. The experience of being fed inappropriately can be uncomfortable, frightening, and aversive. If unable to communicate verbally, the elderly resident may display such behaviors as hitting or spitting in response to the discomfort. Resident aggression has been identified as a predictor of psychological abuse.

We suggest that a lack of training in appropriate feeding techniques can be a contributing factor to force feeding or to feeding little or no food. Force feeding can cause, for example, cuts and abrasions in and around the mouth. This physical harm results in or exacerbates poor oral health, which has been identified as a risk factor for malnutrition and its complications. Feeding little or no food is an obvious risk factor for malnutrition. A commonly cited scenario is a staff member delivering a tray of food to a resident in his or her room, leaving, and then returning some time later and removing the tray, even if the resident has not eaten any of the food.

Syringe Feeding

It must be said that syringe feeding is extremely uncomfortable, hazardous, and frightening to the recipient. To use a syringe for this purpose, the resident must be lying down or reclining with the chin up. This is the worst position in which to swallow. The syringe anchors the tongue so that it cannot be used to control the bolus, and the delivery of (usually thin) puree to the back of the mouth does not allow the resident to prepare to swallow. There is an extremely high probability that the food and liquid will be misdirected into the lungs. This practice is not far removed from the force-feeding of the 19th century "insane asylums," using funnels and hoses. The principle is the same and is abusive (Soriano, 1994). The Ontario College of Nurses has a position statement strongly discouraging this practice as do several state nursing associations. As yet, there is no legislation forbidding it, and it tends to be used more widely than is realized.

Enteral Feeding

Developments in tube feedings and enteral formulae have, indeed, become life savers in certain well-selected patients. It is widely believed that if any patient has difficulty ingesting food by mouth, the answer is to provide enteral feeding, either by nasogastric tube or, more often, by gastrostomy. Unfortunately, in the chronically ill person, this type of feeding does not guarantee adequate nutrition, is easily contaminated, often interacts unfavorably with many medications and, most importantly, causes aspiration pneumonia to a significant degree (Cogen & Weinryb, 1989; Patel & Thomas, 1990; Pick et al., 1996). It exacerbates GER which is then aspirated, usually during sleep, may cause death rapidly or, more often, bacterial pneumonia that cannot be overcome.

Patients with certain types of brain injury do not tolerate enteral feeding (Mitchell, Kiely, & Lipsitz, 1997). Tube feeding for extended periods causes changes in the stomach and short bowel that reduce the ability to absorb nutrients (Peck, Cohen, & Mulvilhill, 1990; Maxtow et al., 1989). Enteral feeding has a high incidence of diarrhea, bloating, nausea, and generalized discomfort. If a patient is malnourished to begin with and develops an infection, such as pneumonia, that requires antibiotic therapy, the medication induces an increased situation of immunocompromise with a downward spiral, sometimes to eventual death. It is currently acknowledged in geriatrics that enteral feeding in the frail, chronically ill elder is contraindicated (Campbell-Taylor & Fisher, 1987; Quill, 1992). This makes it imperative that the patient be fed adequately by mouth.

There is also a misperception that enteral feeding takes less time than oral feeding. If food of the proper consistency and taste is supplied, and staff use the appropriate protocol, it takes less time to feed an equivalent amount of nutrition. If one counts the time spent preparing a feed, gathering equipment, checking gastric residuals, adjusting flow rate, positioning the patient and so on, the amount of time spent by a nurse in relationship to the whole feeding is much greater than that spent feeding a patient by mouth.

Food Thickeners

One recommended procedure for dysphagic patients who choke on thin liquids is to thicken the liquid so that its increased cohesion and weight bring about smoother passage into the esophagus. This approach has, unfortunately, been taken up widely with poor understanding of the dynamics and nutritional processes involved. Commercial thickeners are expensive and difficult to use (Heimburger et al., 1986; Perez & Brandt, 1989). They tend to become too thick if left standing for too long. In order to save costs and to add some nutrition, many facilities use baby cereal, cornstarch, potato flakes, tapioca, and similar substances to thicken liquids. It is not realized that, when one does this, the liquid must then be counted as a food, not part of the patient's daily hydration requirement, because water binds too closely to the thickeners, reducing its availability in the body. Commercial thickeners are made of a substance that releases water readily. The dehydration found in patients on thickened fluids is often attributed to other factors such as kidney failure, rather than to water depletion. Dehydration in the elderly is of particular concern because, with increasing age, the sense of thirst diminishes and less fluid is consumed on a daily basis (Phillips, Rolls, & Ladingam, 1984; Peer, Wigler, & Aviram, 1987). Dehydration tends to cause or increase confusion, delirium and cognitive impairment, exacerbates many cardiac problems, reduces the ability to fight infection, and can lead to death.

Constipation is a significant problem in persons in long-term care and is related to the reduction in fluid intake as well as to inherent problems in the colon. Fiber is often added to the diet without ensuring that sufficient water is given to prevent the formation of obstructive "plugs" of fiber in the gut, thus worsening the constipation (McCargar, Hotson, & Nozza, 1995; Snustad et al., 1991). Laxatives and enemas are then employed, often leading to the loss of vitamins and minerals. Dehydration can also interfere with the action of many medications, either rendering them ineffective or causing unwanted effects because of reduced metabolization and excretion. The half-life of medication, i.e., the time involved up to excretion, tends to be much longer in the elderly under normal conditions. If the patient is dehydrated, the results can be toxicity or overdose (Peer, Wigler, & Aviram, 1987).

MEDICAL, FINANCIAL AND QUALITY OF LIFE CONSEQUENCES OF MALNUTRITION

Costs of Related Acute Illnesses

There is much concern about the aspiration of oral contents as a cause of pneumonia. In fact, many residents can tolerate significant amounts of aspiration for long periods with no ill effects, so long as the lung clearance system and the resident's immune response are sufficient. Immunosuppression is directly related to protein-calorie undernutrition (Lesourd, 1997). Pulmonary infections in chronically ill elders or persons with DD are more often caused by a combination of aspiration of nocturnal reflux causing chemical damage to the lungs, followed by aspirated bacteria from the mouth producing the typical gram-negative pneumonias.

The direct relationship between malnutrition and bedsores that will not heal is of equal concern (Closs, 1993; Pinchcofsky-Devine & Kaminski, 1986). The costs to the system include antibiotics, extra nursing time, acute hospital admissions, and have been calculated as being in excess of $8,000 per patient per illness. Decubiti requiring plastic surgery cost even more. Many, if not most, of these infections could be avoided by maintaining adequate protein-calorie nutrition in the patients. The suffering experienced by the patient can well be imagined and neglect, albeit unintentional, is often involved.

Mortality

It must be kept in mind that while we have described at length the morbidity associated with protein-calorie undernutrition, starvation and dehydration are direct causes of death.

Quality of Life

Malnutrition promotes dependency and a poor quality of life. If a resident is experiencing fatigue, confusion, hunger, thirst, pain, and/or impaired mobility associated with malnutrition and its consequencaes, he or she will likely be unable or unwilling to participate in social and therapeutic programs offered. Furthermore, food itself is a basic necessity of life, and historically, eating has been an important social activity in cultures throughout the world. Loss of the pleasures associated with food and the social experience of eating also has a negative impact on the quality of life of malnourished residents.

SOLUTIONS

Education and Training

Nursing Staff

The argument frequently given as the reason for not being able to provide staff education is cost. There is not only the cost of sending a nursing staff to a course, but he or she must be replaced while on professional leave. Modern technology makes this an indefensible argument. There are videotape training materials available, designed to be used during the regularly scheduled nursing "in-service" time slots, taught by head nurses or nurse clinicians, inexpensive to purchase and usable for all staff on all shifts (Campbell-Taylor, 1995). Some are designed for staff members with little formal education or those who may speak a language other than English.

Administrators, nurse managers, and physicians must become more familiar with the existence and consequences of malnutrition and with methods of establishing its presence. The Nutrition Risk Index, the Maastricht Index and the Mortality Index are all easy to apply and should form the baseline for all residents on admission (Stanek, Po-well, & Betts, 1991; Mion et al., 1994). Residents at particular risk must be identified by physicians and nursing staff together and have individualized nutrition and feeding plans developed. Reassessment at appropriate intervals is essential.

Spoon feeding, if taught and done properly, allows for contact with the resident and increased comfort. It is believed that residents must be fed one-on-one by a staff member and that this condition is what takes so much time. An inappropriate "solution" to this is the "feeding table," a semicircular table with the feeder in the middle and the residents arranged around it. As well as being quite unnatural, the width of the table makes it awkward for the feeder to reach all residents, so that, commonly, the staff member will stand up and move from resident to resident, creating the problem cited above.

If the staff person sits at a table for four (three dependent residents and one staff member) in a normalized environment, as one resident is fed, there is time for the resident to prepare the food for swallowing and swallow the food while the other two residents are receiving food. It eliminates the problem of feeding too quickly and obliges the staff member to sit down. Some residents will always have to be fed by themselves because of distractibility, severe swallowing dysfunction, or other problems. These residents are in the minority. When residents are fed comfortably and at their own pace, the resistive and defensive behaviors often encountered tend to diminish. Studies of residents fed in this manner have demonstrated that residents fed in their rooms by a staff person tend to lose weight while those who eat in a more "normal" environment gain weight.

Physicians

General practitioners, who tend to be medical care providers in long-term care, must become more familiar with the consequences and costs of malnutrition, the effects of medications on the ability to eat, and the important effects of oral health on undernutrition. They must become more familiar with the consequences of enteral feeding in the chronically ill elderly and with the influence of gastroesophageal disorders on the ability to swallow. They should also allot more time to the treatment of long-term care residents (Katz et al., 1997; AAFP, ADA, & NCOA, 1994).

Provision of hydration is often seen to be possible only by intravenous (I.V.) means. This is not only uncomfortable for the resident, but requires, in most locations, that either a physician or an I.V. technician place the tube. This is rarely feasible in the average nursing home. The tube is so uncomfortable that it is constantly pulled out by confused or demented residents and eventually tends to go into the surrounding tissue instead of into the vein with the resident being subjected to the pain of being poked for veins on a regular basis. There is a simpler and much more comfortable solution.

Hypodermoclysis has been used for many years as a means of providing hydration. It fell out of favor in the mid-1960's when I.V. administration of fluids became more popular. It consists of the subcutaneous administration, by slow drip, overnight, of required fluids. A fine needle is inserted under the skin so that is can barely be felt by the resident. The lower abdomen or thigh is the preferred location. Certain medications that can be administered subcutaneously can also be given by this means (Olde Rikkert et al., 1994; Husain & Warshaw, 1996; Rochon et al., 1997). For this reason, it is now commonly used in palliative care. Continuous infusion of morphine is possible by hypodermoclysis (Worobec & Brown, 1997). It can be administered by a nurse or by a home caregiver as it requires even less expertise than intramuscular injection of insulin. Once the flow rate is established, the only difficulty may be swelling at the site of administration. If that happens, the needle simply pops out, is replaced in a different location, and the flow rate readjusted. For the average, dehydrated elderly resident, this may not even be necessary every night; sometimes only three times a week is sufficient.

Pharmacists

Because of the difficulties of administering tablets and capsules to swallowing impaired patients who, worldwide, number in the millions, pharmacists and pharmaceutical companies might well consider the provision of drugs in other forms when possible. Patches, creams, and suppositories would be preferable for medications in which the molecular structure is suitable. Drugs in liquid form can be administered through a temporarily placed oroesophageal tube in patients with little or no gag reflex, the tube being removed after administration of the medication. It takes only a few minutes for the tube to be passed and can be self administered by ambulatory patients and even by some who are mildly demented (Campbell-Taylor et al., 1988). The need for alternate forms of medications is substantial; on the order of the numbers of swallowing impaired patients in hospitals, nursing homes and in the community. It has been determined that, among patients who need to be fed by someone else, over 95% have disorders of swallowing (Siebens et al.,1986). Even asymptomatic older patients have some impairment to varying degrees.

Dietitians

The influence of taste and smell on food consumption needs to be better addressed. As noted before, those who purchase and prepare the food are not those who consume it. It is also a cultural given that sweet foods must necessarily be non-nutritious, even though the most commonly used food supplement is cloyingly sweet to normal palates. Commercially produced, nutrient-dense, adjusted consistency foods are, in the long run, more cost-effective. In countries in which these are not available, dietitians are in the best position to prepare appropriate foods within their given budget. The consistency and viscosity of the food are of paramount importance. For the swallowing impaired resident, it should be of a moist, cohesive texture, without particles that may be inhaled. "Mashed potato" consistency is best for the majority of residents. Liquids and solids are swallowed in different ways, so that food that contains both, e.g., soup with vegetable pieces or dry cereal with milk, should never be served, and liquids should be given separately from solids to avoid the possibility of washing food particles into the lungs. Many nursing homes do not employ dietitians. This is poor economy as, even on a part-time consultation basis, their contribution in terms of clinical nutrition is essential (ADA, 1993; Klein et al., 1997).

Administrators

One of the causes of malnutrition in institutionalized residents is adherence to old practices. One of these is the conviction that we must have three meals a day. As described above, many of these residents suffer from slow gastric emptying. In an ideal situation, they would have several small meals a day. However, under current staffing restrictions as well as kitchen staff requirements, this is not feasible. The next best solution is to take the daily nutritional requirement and divide it into two meals, instead of three. This achieves two things: the resident has time to digest the food and empty the stomach, thus being hungry for the second meal and eating more, and it frees up nursing time. The day and evening shift each have to serve only one meal. This removes another support from the "not enough time" argument. Residents who require and can eat three meals (independent residents) could have access to sandwiches, drinks, soups, etc., at midday. Adherence to a practice that is unsuitable for the majority of residents is not defensible. Although it causes, as do most major changes, resistance and logistical problems with staff responsibilities, union requirements, etc., none of these is sufficient reason not to implement the practice if it will prevent malnutrition in a significant number of residents.

CONCLUSION

Dependent elders and adults with developmental disabilities who must be fed by someone else are particularly vulnerable to neglect and abuse in long-term care settings. Failure to provide adequate nutrition constitutes neglect, and certain identified practices associated with feeding can be abusive.

Undernutrition is a serious and common problem among residents in long-term care facilities and is a significant cause of morbidity, mortality, increased health care costs, and poor quality of life. Multiple interrelated factors contribute to malnutrition and the associated risk of neglect and abuse. These factors are related to the identified conditions common to dependent elderly residents who must be fed by a care provider and to the lack of education and training in the proper protocols required to provide adequate food and liquid to persons with cognitive and physical impairments.

Throughout this article, several protocols have been illustrated. We suggest that these protocols, which are easy to apply with proper training, will decrease malnutrition and the likelihood of staff-patient interactions that could lead to neglect and abuse, and yield a higher quality of life for residents, decrease care provider stress, and reduce costs for nursing home administrators. The interventions described need to be supported by appropriate research.

The need for an interdisciplinary team to provide quality nutritional care, including assessment, care planning, food preparation and feeding, is highlighted. Education and training of nursing staff, physicians, pharmacists, dietitians, and administrators are essential.

Finally, education and training regarding malnutrition and associated neglect and abuse are required for Long-Term Care Ombudsmen who serve to advocate for the highest possible quality of care and quality of life for elderly residents in licensed long-term care facilities throughout the United States.

Food is not only a basic necessity of life. Historically, eating has been an important social activity in cultures throughout the world. As such, nutritional care is an important component of the overall quality of care of residents and impacts significantly on their quality of life. It is essential that dependent residents receive an adequate amount of appropriate and nutritious food and liquid, served in as pleasant and normal an environment as possible, and that they are fed or assisted in eating, to the degree required, in an appropriate, safe, humane, and dignified manner.

REFERENCES

American Dietetic Association (ADA). (1993). Health care reform legislative platform: Economic benefits of nutrition services. *Journal of the American Dietetic Association*, 93, 686-690.

Albibi, R. & McCallum, R.W. (1983). Metoclopramide: Pharmacology and clinical application. *Annals of Internal Medicine*, 98, 86-95.

Aman, M.G. (1990). Considerations in the use of psychotropic drugs in elderly mentally retarded persons. *Journal of Mental Deficiency Research*, 34, 1-10.

American Academy of Family Physicians (AAFP), American Dietetic Association (ADA), National Council on the Aging (NCOA). (1994). *Incorporating Nutrition Screening and Interventions into Medical Practice: A Monograph for Physicians*. Washington, DC: Nutrition Screening Initiative.

Anselmino, M., Zaninotto, G., Costantini, M., Ostuni, P., Ianniello, A., Boccu, C., Doria, A.,Todesco, S., & Ancona, E. (1997). Esophageal motor function in primary Sjogren's syndrome: Correlation with dysphagia and xerostomia. *Digestive Diseases and Sciences, 42*(1), 113-8.

Aviv, J.E., Martin, J.H., Jones, M.E., Wee, T.A., Diamond, B., Keen, M.S., & Blitzer, A. (1994). Age-related changes in pharyngeal and supraglottic sensation. *Annals of Otology, Rhinology, and Laryngology, 10*, 103, 749-52.

Ayres, J.G. & Miles, J.F. (1996). Oesophageal reflux asthma. *European Respiratory Journal*, 9, 1073-78.

Bashford, G. & Bradd, P. (1996). Drug-induced Parkinsonism associated with dysphagia and aspiration: A brief report. *Journal of Geriatric Psychiatry and Neurology*, 9, 133-5.

Bernardi, C. & McGovern, M. (1993). *Nutrition services for improved health and cost savings: Demonstrating success in the District of Columbia.* Washington, DC: District of Columbia Metropolitan Area Dietetic Association.

Boeck, A., Buckley, R.H., & Schiff, R.I. (1997). Gastroesophageal reflux and severe combined immunodeficiency. *Journal of Allergy and Clinical Immunology, 99,* 420-4.

Borgstrom, P.S., Olsson, R., Sundkvist, G. & Ekberg, O. (1988). Pharyngeal and oesophageal function in patients with diabetes mellitus and swallowing complaints. *British Journal of Radiology, 61,* 817-21.

Buchholz, D.W. (1994). Neurogenic dysphagia: What is the cause when the cause is not obvious? *Dysphagia, 9,* 245-55.

Cain, W.S., Reid, F. & Stevens, J.C. (1990). Missing ingredients: Aging and the discrimination of flavor. *Journal of Nutrition for the Elderly, 9,* 3-15.

Campbell-Taylor, I. (1995). *Dysphagia: Feeding strategies for caregivers–Manual and videotape.* Toronto, Canada.

Campbell-Taylor, I. (1996). *Drugs, dysphagia and nutrition. Dietetics in developmental and psychiatric disorders.* American Dietetic Association. January, 1997.

Campbell-Taylor, I. & Fisher, R.H. (1987). The clinical case against tube feeding in palliative care of the elderly. *Journal of the American Geriatrics Society, 35,* 1100-1104.

Campbell-Taylor, I., Nadon, G.W., Sclater, A.L, Fisher, R.H., Harris-Kwan, J. & Rosen, I.E. (1988). Oroesophageal tube feeding: An alternative to nasogastric or gastrostomy tubes. *Dysphagia, 2,* 220-221.

Caruso, A.J. & Max, L. (1997). Effects of aging on neuromotor processes of swallowing. *Seminars in Speech and Language, 18,* 181-92.

Casey, D.E. & Rabius, P. (1978). Tardive dyskinesia as a life-threatening illness. *American Journal of Psychiatry, 135,* 486-488.

Channer, V.S. & Virjee, J.B. (1986). The effect of size and shape of tablets on their esophageal transit. *Journal of Clinical Pharmacology, 26,* 141-146.

Closs, S.J. (1993). Malnutrition: The key to pressure sores? *Nursing Standard, 8,* 32-6.

Coats, K.G., Morgan, S.L., Bartolucci, A.A. & Weinsier, R.L. (1993). Hospital-associated malnutrition: A reevaluation 12 years later. *Journal of the American Dietetic Association, 93,* 27-33.

Cogen, R., Weinryb, J., Pomerantz, C. & Fenstemacher, P. (1991). Complications of jejunostomy tube feeding in nursing facility patients. *American Journal of Gastroenterology, 86,* 1610-1613.

Cogen, R. & Weinryb, J. (1989). Aspiration pneumonia in nursing home patients fed via gastrostomy tubes. *American Journal of Gastroenterology, 84,* 1509-1512.

dePippo, K.L., Holas, M.A., Reding, M.J., Mandel, F.S. & Lesser, M.L. (1994). Dysphagia therapy following stroke: A controlled trial. *Neurology, 4,* 1655-1660.

Disbrow, D.D. & Dowling, R.A. (1991). Cost-effectiveness and cost-benefit analyses: Research to support practice. In E.R. Monsen (ed.), *Research: Successful approaches.* Chicago, IL: American Dietetic Association, 272-294.

Dolan, T.A., Monopoli, M.P., Kaurich, M.J. & Rubenstein, L.Z. (1990). Geriatric grand rounds: Oral diseases in older adults. *Journal of the American Geriatrics Society, 38,* 1239-1250.

Etison, F., Wiart, L., Guatterie, M., Fouillet, N., Lozano, V., Henry, P. & Barat, M. (1996). Effects of central dopaminergic stimulation by apomorphine on swallowing disorders in Parkinson's disease. *Movement Disorders, 11*, 729-32.

Feinberg, M., Kneble, J. & Tully, J. (1989). Pneumonia and aspiration: Findings in an elderly population. Poster presented at the International Congress of Radiology, Paris.

Feinberg, M.J., Kneble, J., Tully, J. and Segall, L. (1990). Aspiration and the elderly. *Dysphagia, 5*, 61-71.

Frantz, R.A., Gardner, S., Harvey, P. & Spacht, J. (1991). The cost of treating pressure ulcers in a long-term care facility. *Decubitus, 4*, 37-42.

Hall, G.R. (1994). Chronic dementia. Challenges in feeding a patient. *Journal of Gerontological Nursing, 20*, 21-30.

Hansel, D.E. & Heinemann, D. (1996). Improving nursing practice with staff education: The challenges of dysphagia. *Gastroenterological Nursing, 19*, 201-6.

Hayashi, T., Nishikawa, T., Koga, I., Uchida, Y. & Yamawaki, S. (1997). Life-threatening dysphagia following prolonged neuroleptic therapy. *Clinical Neuropharmacology, 20*, 77-81.

Heimburger, D.C, Yung, V.R., Bistrian, B.R., Ettinger, W.H., Jr., Lipschitz, D.A. & Rudman, D. (1986). The role of protein in nutrition, with particular reference to the composition and use of enteral feeding formulas. A consensus report. *Journal of Parenteral and Enteral Nutrition, 10*, 425-30.

Hildebrandt, G.H., Dominguez, B.L., Schork, M.A. & Loesche, W.J. (1997). Functional units, chewing, swallowing, and food avoidance among the elderly. *Journal of Prosthetic Dentistry, 77*, 588-95.

Hirota, K., Yoneyama, T., Ota, M..Hashimoto, K. & Miyake, Y. (1997). Pharyngeal bacteria and professional oral health care in elderly people. *Nippon Ronen Igakkai Zasshi, 34*, 125-9.

Holzapfel, S.K., Ramirez, R.F., Layton, M.S., Smith, I.W., Sagl-Massey, K. & DuBose, J.Z (1996). Feeder position and food and fluid consumed by nursing home residents. *Journal of Gerontological Nursing, 22*, 6-12.

Horn, J.R. (1996). Use of prokinetic agents in special populations. *American Journal of Health-Systems Pharmacy, 53*, S27-9.

Hussain, N.A. & Warshaw, G. (1996). Utility of clysis for hydration in nursing home residents. *Journal of the American Geriatrics Society, 44*, 969-73.

Huttenbrink, K.B. (1995). Disorders of the sense of smell and taste. *Therapeutisch Umschaw, 52*, 732-7.

Intintoli, A.M. & Woulfin, D. (1990). Are you feeding the patient or the garbage can? *Journal of Nutrition for the Elderly, 9*, 63-8.

Kagami, H., Hayashi, T., Shigetomi, T. & Ueda, M. (1995). Assessment of the effects of aging and medication on salivary gland function in patients with xerostomia using 99mTC-scintigraphy. *Nagoya Journal of Medical Science, 58*, 149-55.

Katz, P.R., Karuza, J., Kolassa, J. & Hutson, A. (1997). Medical practice with nursing home residents. *Journal of the American Geriatrics Society, 45*, 911-916.

Klein, S., Kinney, J., Jeejeebhoy, K., Alpers, D., Hellerstein, M., Murray, M. & Twomey, P. (1997). Nutrition support in clinical practice: Review of published data and recommendations for future research directions. National Institutes of

Health, American Society for Parenteral and Enteral Nutrition, and American Society for Clinical Nutrition. *Journal of Parenteral and Enteral Nutrition, 21,* 133-56.

Lamey, P.J., Darwazeh, A.M. & Frier, B.M. (1992). Oral disorders associated with diabetes mellitus. *Diabetes Medicine, 9,* 410-6.

Lamprecht, A. (1990). Dysarthria, dysphagia or dyspnea as a reason for the initial consultation in pseudoparalytic myasthenia gravis and amyotrophic lateral sclerosis. *Laryngorhinootologie, 69,* 48-51.

Lenander-Lumikari, M. & Johansson, I. (1995). Effect of saliva composition on growth of Candida albicans and Torulopsis glabrata. *Oral Microbiology and Immunology, 10,* 233-40.

Lipschitz, D.A. (1991). Malnutrition in the elderly. *Seminars in Dermatology, 10,* 273-81.

Leopold, N.A. (1996). Dysphagia in drug-induced parkinsonism: A case report. *Dysphagia, 11,* 151-3.

Leopold, N.A. & Kagel, M.C. (1997). Pharyngo-esophageal dysphagia in Parkinson's disease. *Dysphagia, 12,* 11-8; discussion 19-20.

Lesourd, B.M. (1997). Nutrition and immunity in the elderly: Modification of immune responses with nutritional treatments. *American Journal of Clinical Nutrition, 66,* 478S-484S.

Loesche, W.J. (1991). Role of anaerobic bacteria in periodontal disease. *Annals of Otology, Rhinology, and Laryngology, Supplement, 154,* 43-5.

Lynch, D.P. (1994). Oral candidiasis. History, classification, and clinical presentation. *Oral Surgical, Oral Medical and Oral Pathology, 78,* 189-93.

Manson, A. & Shea, S. (1991). Malnutrition in elderly ambulatory medical patients. *American Journal of Public Health, 8,* 1195-7.

Maxton, D.G., Menzies, I.S., Slavin, B. & Thompson, R.P. (1989). Small-intestinal function during enteral feeding and starvation in man. *Clinical Science, 77,* 401-6.

McCargar, L.J., Hotson, B.L. & Nozza, A. (1995). Fibre and nutrient intakes of chronic care elderly patients. *Journal of Nutrition for the Elderly, 15,* 13-30.

Meyer, D., Hartmann, K. & Kuhn, M. (1996). Drug-induced taste disorders. *Schweiz Rundsch Med Prax, 85,* 1468-72.

Mion, L.C., McDowell, J.A. & Heaney, L.K. (1994). Nutritional assessment of the elderly in the ambulatory care setting. *Nurse Practitioner Forum, 5,* 46-51.

Mitchell, S.L., Kiely, D.K. & Lipsitz, L.A. (1997). The risk factors and impact on survival of feeding tube placement in nursing home residents with severe cognitive impairment. *Archives of Internal Medicine, 157,* 327-32.

Nelson, K.J., Coulston, A.M., Sucher, K.P. & Tseng, R.Y. (1993). Prevalence of malnutrition in the elderly admitted to long-term-care facilities. *Journal of the American Dietetic Association, 93,* 459-461.

Niedermeier, W.H. & Kramer, R. (1992). Salivary secretion and denture retention. *Journal of Prosthetic Dentistry, 67,* 211-216.

Nilsson, H., Ekberg, O., Olsson, R. & Hindfelt, B. (1996). Quantitative assessment of oral and pharyngeal function in Parkinson's disease. *Dysphagia, 11,* 144-50.

Nompleggi, D., Bell, S.J., Blackburn, G.L. & Bistrian, B.R. (1989). Overview of gastrointestinal disorders due to diabetes mellitus: Emphasis on nutritional support. *Journal of Parenteral and Enteral Nutrition, 13*, 84-91.

Olde Rikkert, M.G., Bogaers, M.A. & Bruijns, E. (1994). Hypodermoclysis, an undervalued rehydration method in geriatrics *Tijdschrift Voor Gerontologie en Geriatrie*, 25(5), 197-204.

Olin, A.O., Osterberg, P., Hadell, K., Armyr, I., Jerstrom, S. & Ljungqvist, O. (1996). Energy-enriched hospital food to improve energy intake in elderly patients. *Journal of Parenteral and Enteral Nutrition, 20*, 93-97.

Osborn, C.L. & Marshall, M.J. (1993). Self-feeding performance in nursing home residents. *Journal of Gerontological Nursing, 19*, 7-14.

Ouslander, J.G. (1981). Drug therapy in the elderly. *Annals of Internal Medicine, 95*, 711-22.

Parkman, H.P. & Fisher, R.S. (1997). Contributing role of motility abnormalities in the pathogenesis of gastroesophageal reflux disease. *Digestive Disorders and Sciences, Supplement 1*, 40-52.

Patel, A.H. & Thomas, E. (1990). Risk factors for pneumonia after percutaneous endoscopic gastrostomy. *Journal of Clinical Gastroenterology, 12*, 389-392.

Paton, R., Huber, R. & Netting, F.E. (1994). The Long-Term Care Ombudsman Program and complaints of abuse and neglect: What have we learned? *Journal of Elder Abuse & Neglect, 6*, 97-115.

Peck, A., Cohen, C.E., & Mulvihill, M.N. (1990). Long-term enteral feeding of aged demented nursing home patients. *Journal of the American Geriatrics Society, 38*, 1195-1198.

Peer, G., Wigler, I. & Aviram, A. (1987). Prolonged volume depletion imitating end-stage renal failure. *American Journal of the Medical Sciences, 294*, 214-7.

Perez, S.K. & Brandt, K. (1989). Enteral feeding contamination: Comparison of diluents and feeding bag usage. *Journal of Parenteral and Enteral Nutrition, 13*, 306-308.

Phillips, P.A., Rolls, B.J. & Ladingam, J.G. (1984). Reduced thirst after water deprivation in healthy elderly men. *New England Journal of Medicine, 311*, 753-755.

Pick, N., McDonald, A., Bennett, N., Litsche, M., Dietsche, L., Legerwood, R., Spurgas, R. & LaForce, F.M. (1996). Pulmonary aspiration in a long-term care setting: Clinical and laboratory observations and an analysis of risk factors. *Journal of the American Geriatrics Society, 44*, 763-8.

Pillemer, K. & Moore, D.E. (1990). Highlights from a study of abuse of patients in nursing homes. *Journal of Elder Abuse & Neglect, 2*, 5-29.

Pinchcofsky-Devin, G.D. & Kaminski, M.V. (1986). Correlation of pressure sores and nutritional status. *Journal of the American Geriatrics Society, 34*, 435- 440.

Poewe, W.H., Lees, A.J. & Stern, G.M. (1988). Dystonia in Parkinson's disease: Clinical and pharmacological features. *Annals of Neurology, 23*, 73-8.

Priefer, B.A. & Robbins, J. (1997). Eating Changes in Mild-Stage Alzheimer's Disease: A Pilot Study. *Dysphagia, 12*, 212-221.

Poothullil, J.M. (1995). Regulation of nutrient intake in humans: A theory based on taste and smell. *Neuroscience and Behavioral Reviews, 19*, 407-12.

Quigley, E.M. (1996). Gastrointestinal dysfunction in Parkinson's disease. *Seminars in Neurology, 16*, 245-50.

Quill, T.E. (1992). Utilization of nasogastric feeding tubes in a group of chronically ill, elderly patients in a community hospital. *Dysphagia, 7*, 64-70.

Raventos, J.M., Kralemann, H. & Gray, D.B. (1982). Mortality risks of mentally retarded and mentally ill patients after a feeding gastrostomy. *American Journal of Mental Deficiency, 86*, 439-444.

Rhodus, N.L. (1990). Nutritional intake in both free-living and institutionalized older adults with xerostomia. *Journal of Nutrition & the Elderly, 10*, 1-32.

Richter, J.E., Wu, W.C., Johns, D.N., Blackwell, J.N., Nelson, J.L., Castell, J.A. & Castell, D.O. (1987). Esophageal manometry in 95 healthy adult volunteers. Variability of pressures with age and frequency of "abnormal" contractions. *Digestive Diseases and Science, 32*, 583-92.

Robbins, J., Levine, R., Wood, J., Roecker, E.B. & Luschei, E. (1995). Age effects on lingual pressure generation as a risk factor for dysphagia. *Journal of Gerontology Series A Biological Sciences Medical Sciences, 50*, 57-62.

Robinson, G., Goldstein, M. & Levine, G. (1987). Impact of nutritional status on DRG length of stay. *Journal of Parenteral and Enteral Nutrtion, 11*, 49-51.

Rochon, P.A., Gill, S.S., Litner, J., Fischbach, M., Goodison, A.J. & Gordon, M. (1997). A systematic review of the evidence for hypodermoclysis to treat dehydration in older people. *Journal of Gerontology Series A Biology Sciences and Medical Sciences, 52*(3), M169-76.

Sanders, H.N. (1990). Feeding dependent eaters among geriatric patients. *Journal of Nutrition the Elderly, 9*, 69-74.

Sciubba, J.J. (1994). Sjogren's syndrome: Pathology, oral presentation, and dental management. *Compendium, 15*(9), 1084, 1086.

Sciubba, J.J. (1996). Opportunistic oral infections in the immunosuppressed patient: Oral hairy leukoplakia and oral candidiasis. *Advances in Dental Research, 10*, 69-72.

Ship, J.A., Pearson, J.D., Cruise, L.J., Brant, L.J. & Metter, E.J. (1996). Longitudinal changes in smell indentification. *Journal of Gerontology Series A Biological Sicences Medical Sciences, 51*, M86-91.

Ship, J.A., Duffy, V., Jones, J.A. & Langmore, S. (1996). Geriatric oral health and its impact on eating. *Journal of the American Geriatrics Society, 44*, 456-64.

Siebens, H., Trupe, E., Siebens, A., Cook, F., Anshen, S., Hanauer, R. & Oster, G. (1986). Correlates and consequences of eating dependency in institutionalized elderly. *Journal of the American Geriatrics Society, 34*, 192-8.

Smithard, D.G., O'Neill, P.A., Parks, C. & Morris, J. (1996). Complications and outcome after acute stroke. Does dysphagia matter? *Stroke, 27*,1200-4.

Snustad, D., Lee, V., Abraham, I., Alexander, C., Bella, D. & Cumming, C. (1991). Dietary fiber in hospitalized geriatric patients: Too soft a solution for too hard a problem? *Journal of Nutrition for the Elderly, 10*, 49-63.

Soriano, R. (1994). Syringe feeding: Current clinical practice and recommendations. *Geriatric Nursing, 15*, 85-7.

Stanek, K., Powell, C. & Betts, N. (1991). Nutritional knowledge of nurses in long-term health care facilities. *Journal of Nutrition for the Elderly, 10*, 35-48.

Stevens, J.C., Cruz, L.A., Hoffman, J.M. & Patterson, M.Q. (1995). Taste sensitivity and aging: High incidence of decline revealed by repeated threshold measures. *Chemical Senses, 20,* 451-9.

Sundkvist, G., Hillarp, B., Lilja, B. & Ekberg, O. (1989). Esophageal motor function evaluated by scintigraphy, video-radiography and manometry in diabetic patients. *Acta Radiologica, 30,* 17-9.

Swagerty, D.L., Jr. (1995). Malnutrition in the elderly. *Kansas Medicine, 96,* 182-4.

Triadafilopoulos, G., Hallstone, A., Nelson-Abbott, H. & Bedinger, K. (1992). Oropharyngeal and esophageal interrelationships in patients with nonobstructive dysphagia. *Digestive Disease and Sciences, 37,* 551-7.

US Agency for Health Care Policy and Research, Public Health Service (AHCPR). (1991). *Salivary electrostimulation in Sjogren's Syndrome.* U.S. Department of Health and Human Services Publication #AHCPR 91-0009.

US General Accounting Office (GAO). (1998). *California nursing homes: Care problems persist despite federal and state oversight.* Washington, DC: US Government Printing Office.

US Senate Special Committee on Aging. (1997). *The risk of malnutrition in nursing homes.* Washington, DC: US Government Printing Office.

Vissink, A., Spijkervet, F.K. & Van Nieuw Amerongen, A. (1996). Aging and saliva: A review of the literature. *Special Care in Dentistry, 16,* 95-103.

Wang, S.Y., Fukagawa, N., Hossain, M. & Ooi, W.L. (1997). Longitudinal weight changes, length of survival, and energy requirements of long term care residents with dementia. *Journal of the American Geriatrics Society, 45,* 1189-1895.

Wenning, G.K., Shephard, B., Hawkes, C., Petruckevitch, A., Lees, A. & Quinn, N. (1995). Olfactory function in atypical parkinsonian syndromes. *Acta Neurologia Scandinavia, 91,* 247-50.

Woo, P. C., Noordzij, P. & Ross, J.A. (1996). Association of esophageal reflux and globus symptom: Comparison of laryngoscopy and 24-hour pH manometry. *Otolaryngology and Head and Neck Surgery, 115,* 502-7.

Worobec, G. & Brown, M.K. (1997). Hypodermoclysis therapy in a chronic care hospital setting. *Journal of Gerontological Nursing, 23,* 23-8.

Yamagishi, M., Takami, S., Getchell, T.V. (1995). Innervation in human taste buds and its decrease in Alzheimer's disease patients. *Acta Otolaryngologia (Stockholm), 115,* 678-84.

Zahler, L.P., Holdt, C.S., Gates, G.E. & Keiser, A.V. (1993). Nutritional care of ambulatory residents in special care units for Alzeimer's patients. *Journal of Nutrition for the Elderly, 12,* 5-19.

Zou, Z., Zhang, Z. & Hua, H. (1995). Sialographic follow-up study of patients with Sjogren's syndrome. *Chinese Medical Journal (English), 108,* 528-34.

A Fit Person to Run a Home:
Registered Homes Tribunal Interpretations
of the 'Fit Person' Concept
in the United Kingdom

Alison Brammer, BA (Hons)

SUMMARY. The abuse of people living in residential care in the UK is well documented. A further wealth of information is available in the form of anecdotal accounts of those who have been employed in this sector but who, in a climate which is still somewhat hostile to 'whistle blowers,' are not prepared to formally report their concerns. A small but significant amount of hard evidence of abuse exists in the reports of the Registered Homes Tribunal decisions. This body has the jurisdiction to hear appeals concerning the running of registered and nursing homes in the UK. The circumstances portrayed range from issues of 'bad practice' to abuse which may be physical, psychological, or sexual, perpetrated by staff, home owners, residents, or visitors. Many of the cases which concern the tribunal focus on whether a given individual is a 'fit person' to run a home. It is the aim of this article to consider and reflect on the tribunals' interpretation of that term, in relation to the operation and decisions of the tribunal. *[Article copies available for a fee from The Haworth Document Delivery Service: 1-800-342-9678. E-mail address: getinfo@haworthpressinc.com]*

KEYWORDS. Regulations, process, precedent, evidence, elder abuse

---

Alison Brammer is Lecturer in Law, Keele University, School and Department of Law, Keele, Staffordshire, ST5 5BG, UK. She is also Solicitor of the Supreme Court.

[Haworth co-indexing entry note]: "A Fit Person to Run a Home: Registered Homes Tribunal Interpretations of the 'Fit Person' Concept in the United Kingdom." Brammer, Alison. Co-published simultaneously in *Journal of Elder Abuse & Neglect* (The Haworth Maltreatment & Trauma Press, an imprint of The Haworth Press, Inc.) Vol. 10, No. 1/2, 1999, pp. 119-131; and: *Elder Abuse and Neglect in Residential Settings: Different National Backgrounds and Similar Responses* (ed: Frank Glendenning, and Paul Kingston) The Haworth Press, Inc., 1999, pp. 119-131. Single or multiple copies of this article are available for a fee from The Haworth Document Delivery Service [1-800-342-9678, 9:00 a.m. - 5:00 p.m. (EST). E-mail address: getinfo@haworthpressinc.com].

119

BACKGROUND:
REGULATION OF RESIDENTIAL CARE
IN THE UNITED KINGDOM (UK)

A formal system of residential care regulation in the UK was introduced with the passing of the Registered Homes Act of 1984, in response to the significant expansion in private sector care at that time. The Act also established the Registered Homes Tribunal. Regulation operates through the registration and inspection functions invested in the registration authority. For registered homes (residential care) this is the local authority 'arms length' inspection unit, whereas for nursing homes it is the health authority. Some homes are dual registered and can thus offer both registered and nursing accommodation. Higher ages and dependency levels of those entering residential accommodation support a move towards a single category care home which would ensure more consistent standards, reduce duplication of effort, and avoid the need for residents to move at a time when their care needs are increasing (Hoyes & Johnson, 1997). This is just one of the issues currently under discussion in a consultation exercise that aims to review the regulation of social services in England and Wales (DH, 1992, 1995; Burgner, 1996). The framework for regulation of registered and nursing homes is largely similar. Throughout this article the focus will be on the legislation applicable to registered homes unless otherwise stated.

The requirement of registration is imposed on "any establishment which provides . . . residential accommodation with both board and personal care for persons in need of personal care by reason of old age, disablement, past or present dependence on alcohol or drugs, or past or present mental disorder" [S. 1 Registered Homes Act 1984 (the Act)]. It is an offence to operate a home without registration (s. 2); and registration is personal to the proprietor (and manager, if appropriate) rather than being attached to the property. The National Health Service and Community Care Act of 1990 heralded greater emphasis on provision of care to enable individuals to live independently in the community. There will, nevertheless, remain a significant number of people who require residential and nursing accommodation. The vast majority of residents are elderly; however, there are indications that the number of adults with learning disabilities in need of accommodation is growing (Parrott et al., 1997). Abuse of this client group is also evident and has recently been the subject of an independent inquiry in Buckinghamshire (BCC, 1998).

POWERS OF THE REGISTRATION AUTHORITY

The registration authority must consider applications for registration and has the power to refuse an application. The grounds for refusal are specified in s. 9 and include circumstances when a person concerned in operating the home is not a fit person, or that premises are not fit to be used as a home, or that reasonable services or facilities will not be provided. Existing registration may be canceled, under the grounds for refusal ab initio, including the fit person criteria, or non-payment of the annual registration fee, or discovery of a "relevant conviction" of the registered person (s.10). In emergencies there is a separate, speedier procedure for cancellation, where circumstances present a serious risk to the life, health, or well-being of residents (s.11). The registration authority may attach conditions to registration although this power is limited to specification of the number, age, sex, and category of residents (s.5(3)). To carry out its regulatory function, registration authorities have the power to enter and inspect premises (s.17) and must inspect at least twice a year with one of these visits being unannounced (Reg. 18(1) Residential Care Homes Regulations, 1984).

It is also evident that part of the role of the inspection body is to offer support and guidance to care home operators and suggest ways to improve practice over time (see for example, Fallon v Lancashire County Council (1992) Decision 208). The potential for conflict where the inspector is invested with functions of both trainer and regulator has been noted (Brammer, 1994). The Burgner report (1996) warns 'there are limits to what can be achieved–indeed to what should be attempted–through the inspection process. If ensuring that basic registration standards are being met (the policing function) is the core of the inspection process, this sets limits to how far inspectors can pursue a broader advisory role . . . Advice has to stop well short of a full-blown consultancy function, since inspectors cannot both advise providers and then formally inspect the results of their advice' (p. 76).

For less serious breaches of the regulations, which would not warrant closure of a home, the magistrates court has jurisdiction to hear criminal prosecutions brought by the registration authority when a registered person has failed to comply with a notice requiring action to remedy the breach. These regulations cover such matters as the conduct of homes (reg. 9) which includes making 'proper provision for the welfare, care, and, where appropriate, treatment and supervision of all residents (reg. 9(1)); provision of facilities and services (reg. 10), which includes employing suitably qualified staff, providing suitable furniture, adequate light and heating; taking adequate precautions against risk of fire and accident, supplying suitable food, and maintaining a variety of records (reg. 6). It has been noted that the regulations are somewhat vague and much is worded in terms of 'adequacy' rather than quality (Brammer, 1996). This subjective element may make it practically very difficult to satisfy the criminal standard of proof required in the magistrates court.

THE TRIBUNAL

The Registered Homes Tribunal is a specialist body that deals exclusively with matters relating to the registration, de-registration, and general operation of care homes (registered and nursing). In the 13 years since its introduction (on 1st January 1985, the implementation date of the 1984 Act) it has dealt with a relatively small number of cases. As of July 1998, only 340 case reports have been published. A similar number of cases have been directed to the tribunal but resolved prior to a hearing. It might be suggested from these figures that there must be a high level of good practice in care homes. It must be acknowledged, however, that the tribunal's remit is to deal with 'appeals' against the decisions of registration authorities. There must be a significant number of cases where the registration authority's decision to refuse registration or to cancel registration is accepted outright by the registered person. Such cases would not come to the attention of the tribunal. In the future we may see even less recourse to the tribunal if a mediation and arbitration service to settle disputes informally is introduced (Burgner, 1996).

MATTERS OF PROCESS

The tribunal comprises a legally qualified chair and two expert 'wing' members from the private and public sector. The Registered

Homes Tribunal Rules (1984) prescribe the procedure to be followed, the tribunal retaining a residual discretion. The proceedings will normally be held in public and situated in a variety of venues around the country from council chambers and town halls to schools and even a castle. The whole ethos behind the introduction of tribunals into the English legal system was to provide a specialist forum to deal with particular disputes in a speedy and less formal manner than the courts system. The Registered Homes Tribunal has not satisfied either of these aims. Delays of up to 18 months between registration authority notice and the tribunal hearing have occurred. It is significant that in the interim the home will continue to operate. In some cases at the tribunal's instigation, preliminary meetings have been held to discuss procedural matters in advance, and there has been mutual exchange of witness statements (see, for example, Henshaw v Trafford Borough Council (1996) Decision 310). The introduction of these and other steps as formal requirements has been suggested to speed up and strengthen the process (Burgner, 1996.) Most hearings have a high degree of formality. Although there is no provision for legal aid, perhaps because of the issues at stake, home owners are usually legally represented. This instills an adversarial and legalistic tone to the proceedings. The implications of these factors are clearly summarised, "The delays are frustrating and can be unfair to providers as well as putting vulnerable witnesses at risk. Costs are high and this may deter both sides from using the tribunal" (Burgner, p. 74).

PRECEDENT

The Divisional Court and the Court of Appeal hear appeals against decisions of the tribunal. Few cases have proceeded to this stage; those that do so focus on matters of law or interpretation of the statute (see: Harrison v Cornwall County Council (1991) 90 L.G.R.81, Lyons v East Sussex County Council (1988) 86 LGR 369, R v Humberside County Council, ex parte Bogdal (1992) COD 467). The tribunal itself is not bound by its own previous decisions. Rideout (1998) argues that "tribunal decisions, whilst "interesting and illuminating," should be approached with caution and . . . regarded, at the highest, as mildly persuasive" (pp. 18-19). The tribunal itself appeared to share this view, in rejecting references to earlier decisions and stating, "each appeal is based on different facts and has to be decided on its own individual merits" (Taylor v East Sussex County Council (1992) Decision 191). Ridout argues this approach is necessary to allow for changing circumstances and practices and prevent the tribunal being restricted by a decision set in a different historic context. The same argument could apply, however, to almost any area of law and is generally avoided by distinguishing the facts of particular cases. The view of Burgner is preferable. He acknowledges that, "the decisions do not form a binding precedent"; their value lies, however, in the fact that, "through a growing body of case law they provide guidance about what might be considered acceptable or unacceptable from a registration authority. Their decisions tend to shape the views of inspection units about what they can ask from providers, and they offer protection to providers from unreasonable demands by regulators." This view is supported in the case of Richardson v Norfolk County Council (1986) (Decision 44). Reference was made to decision 1 where, "The facts were different, but what was said as a matter of principle still holds good as a guideline on policy."

EVIDENCE

Cases before the tribunal are decided in accordance with the civil standard of proof. The burden of proof lies on the party asserting a particular fact. Registration authorities must therefore prove that an individual is not a fit person; it is not for the individual concerned to prove his or her fitness. Evidence must be adduced which satisfies the tribunal on 'a balance of probabilities.' In Lyons v East Sussex (above) the tribunal determined that a heavier burden than 'balance of probabilities' could apply and the degree of probability may vary depending on the seriousness of the case. This was applied in Bissondial Singh Seeckun v Plymouth Health Authority (1994) (Decision 243) where it was decided that the appellant was not a fit person having falsely represented unqualified staff as qualified. The tribunal noted the seriousness of the matter for the appellant. "The Home will probably have to be disposed of. . . . and his livelihood may be jeopardised. Most importantly, his reputation will be shattered. . . . .It is therefore essential that the evidence should be cogent, weighty and persuasive to a high degree" (see also: Mitchell v West Sussex County Council (1991) Decision 162). It is an approach that could work against the interests of the residents whom the legislation is designed to offer protection. The case of Marie Louis Anthony Esq. v Isle of Wight County Council (1995) (Decision 261) clearly illustrates this point. It was contended that the appellant was unfit because he failed to inform the council of a serious incident, the over medication of a resident; failed to keep accurate records; was hostile towards officers; responded aggressively to complaints; and failed to employ suitably competent and qualified staff. The tribunal found that on balance of probability it had sufficient doubts to decide that the appellant was unfit, yet it was not satisfied of this on a higher standard of proof. The appellant therefore succeeded in his appeal.

Effectively, this interpretation means that the more serious an allegation that is made against an operator, e.g., an assault of which a resident is a victim, the more difficult it is to prove. It is precisely because many such matters are difficult to prove to such a high standard that there are few criminal prosecutions against individuals in this area. In a context where the aim of the legislation is to protect vulnerable residents, it is argued that higher standards of proof should remain the domain of the criminal courts.

INSPECTORS' APPROACHES TO 'FITNESS'

Cases brought before the tribunal have been subject to a decision that is made by the registration authority on the recommendation of an officer from the inspection unit. It is the inspector, therefore, who makes the initial assessment as to 'fitness' or other relevant grounds. One of the major criticisms of regulation in this area relates to the lack of consistency between areas and inspection teams in terms of both organisation and practice (Counsel and Care, 1995). It would, perhaps, not be surprising to see this inconsistency echoed in tribunal decisions. National guidance was published in 1991 when inspection units, previously located within local authority social services departments, moved to become 'arms length' inspection units (SSI, 1991). The need to reduce variance remains, however, and to this end national training programmes for inspectors may be introduced in the future. The variance in approach is explicit in the range of methods employed by health authorities to assess 'fitness' revealed in a survey conducted by the Royal College of Nursing in 1994 (An inspector calls?). In ascertaining 'fitness' of the registered person: 90% requested references, 77% undertook a police check, 67% interviewed the applicant; 42%

checked finances of the applicant, 17% requested a detailed curriculum vitae, 14% requested a statement about health, 14% requested a business plan, and 6% instituted a company search. It follows that 10% of respondents failed even to take up references. One authority admitted they carried out no assessment of the person seeking to be registered. It is difficult to think of a comparable profession, where an individual can hold a position with such a level of responsibility for others, that would tolerate such laxity in its approach to suitability for membership. It is true that many inspection units are over stretched and under staffed; however, the true cost of providing an effective inspection service with sufficient staff levels must be set against the costs of monitoring 'unsuitable' home owners and the cost of recourse to the tribunal. To complement and enhance the work of inspection units, lay assessors are now included in certain inspections. Reports of inspections provide further insight into the work of the inspection unit and can be viewed as public documents.

FIT PERSON–THE DECISIONS

An early decision of the tribunal gave a clear description of the qualities it sought in assessing 'fitness.' "There is no statutory definition of a "fit" or "unfit" person. It is probably easier to recognise the quality of fitness than to attempt to define it. However the words "trust," "integrity," "uprightness," "honourable," and "truthful," spring to mind. A fit person is one who can be trusted, in whom one has confidence, who acts according to high principles. It follows that a person will be unfit if he or she is untrustworthy or dishonest" (Azzopardi v London Borough of Havering (1988) Decision 76). This statement has been cited in subsequent decisions, perhaps not surprisingly since there is an absence of clear statutory or official guidance on the meaning of the term. Ridout (1998) suggests that the term 'fit' is synonymous with 'suitable' that may, as he argues, simplify the task; however, it remains a highly subjective term. Consideration of a cross section of decisions illustrates the range of qualities of fitness and unfitness adjudicated by the tribunal. Analysis of the decisions supports the need for the introduction of guidance in the form of a checklist of factors applicable in assessing fitness.

Many of the tribunal decisions consider issues linking criminality and unfitness. Included are cases where the registered person has a criminal record, is associated with a person who has a criminal record, or employs people with a criminal record. There is no automatic bar to registration as a result of a criminal offence, and the tribunal has been willing to assess the nature of criminality and determine its bearing on the individual's fitness to be concerned in running a home. It may be argued that this is a generous approach when the elements of the role are considered together with the vulnerability of residents. In assessing fitness, it would have been good practice by the registration authority to request disclosure of previous criminal convictions; the power to require disclosure was only introduced in 1991 by the Residential Care Homes (Amendment) Regulations 1991. Proprietors and managers are obliged to provide details of any previous convictions. The value of this provision is illustrated in Conroy v Lancashire County Council (1996) Decision 298, when the appellant made a false declaration claiming she had no previous convictions in her application for registration. The police check revealed convictions for theft and obtaining money by false pretences. A dangerous loophole remains: for other staff employed in the home, there is no mechanism to insist on disclosure of previous convictions. It is hoped that the proposed introduction of a new Social Care Register may bolster this omission.

In the first case under the Act, Beilby v Sefton Metropolitan Borough Council (1985) Decision 1, the tribunal unanimously refused the appeal of Mrs. Beilby, who was found to be unfit due to her conviction for theft from a previous employer. Although it was noted that she was of 'exemplary character,' the tribunal was concerned that she had stolen when in a position of trust and this could not equate with the high standard of integrity required of staff in a residential care home. This contrasts with a decision later in the same year, Phillips v Peterborough Health Authority (1985) Decision 6. Here, the appellant owner's appeal against refusal of registration was allowed. She had been convicted for personation in the parliamentary election and sentenced to two months imprisonment. The tribunal felt that although it was an offence of dishonesty, Mrs. Phillips had gained no personal benefit and residents were unlikely to be adversely affected by her registration. The tribunal contrasted the situation where there was personal gain from a dishonesty offence and confined its decision to the particular facts of the case.

The tribunal is not confined to consideration of criminal behaviour which is prosecuted in the criminal courts. In Janet Evans v West Glamorgan Health Authority (1995) Decision 264 the appellant stole jewelry from a deceased resident, some of which she sold, and the remainder she was seen wearing. The reasons given by the Crown Prosecution Service for not prosecuting were that the appellant had not directly benefited from the proceeds of the sale. Additional reasons supporting a finding of unfitness in this case were that the appellant had obtained an antibiotic drug from a pharmacist without prescription and instructed staff to administer it to a patient.

Abuse of elderly and vulnerable adults takes many forms. Arguably the most difficult to recognise and prove is sexual. Inappropriate sexual behaviour by a home owner, though not directed towards a resident, had a bearing on fitness in Philip J Godfrey Esq. v Kent County Council (1995) Decision 275. The home owner indecently assaulted a member of the staff who was sleeping on night duty at the home. The tribunal stated that the offence, "gave rise to grave concern as to his behaviour towards staff, his ability to observe appropriate boundaries and the abuse of power." It was also significant in this case that he failed to disclose the offence to the registration authority. In Mitchell v West Sussex County Council (1991) Decision 162, an appeal against cancellation was successful in a case where there was an allegation that the proprietor had sexual intercourse with an elderly, mentally handicapped female resident. The registration authority believed the account of the resident and her consistent recollection of events and canceled registration on the basis that even if she gave her consent, Mr. Mitchell's behaviour breached the trust that should exist between resident and proprietor. The tribunal, however was clearly impressed by Mr. Mitchell, considered it unlikely that he would find the resident attractive, and were not convinced to a high standard of proof that the allegations were true. Such an approach is unlikely to encourage residents to come forward with allegations and may leave them feeling that by doing so they will have everything to lose and nothing to gain. In a more recent case, the risk of inappropriate sexual behaviour based on prior conduct was sufficient to justify cancellation of registration of a small home in Gregson v Lancashire County Council (1997) Decision 312. The owner had been dismissed from his previous employment as a nurse for gross misconduct which involved sexual assault on a patient both in hospital and after her return home. Again it was significant that the appellant had attempted to withhold this information from the registration authority.

Registration authorities have limited powers to attach conditions to registration. Breach of such conditions is not only a discrete ground for cancellation, but it may also present a clear indication that the person is unfit. In Piper v Birmingham City Council (1989) Decision 118, the proprietor was found to be unfit for exceeding the maximum number of residents specified in her registration. In that case there was no evidence of abuse. It is perhaps implicit, however, that care standards may fall if there are a greater number of residents accommodated than specifically permitted.

Standards in care homes obviously vary. The range of circumstances depicted in cases illustrate inconsistencies with all of the values advocated in 1989 guidance, *Homes Are For Living In*; namely, privacy, dignity, independence, choice, rights, and fulfillment. Many early decisions concerned multiple occupancy of rooms which may compromise the right to privacy and conflict with the advice given in *Home Life* (1984) that single rooms are preferable. In one instance a man and woman were placed in shared accommodations, even though the woman was unable to give informed consent to the arrangement (Lackundeo Nursing Esq. v Hampshire County Council (1992) Decision 200). In Gilead v Leicestershire County Council (1987) Decision 54, the appellants were granted three years to phase out three bedded rooms. More recently, in Henshaw v Trafford Borough Council (1996) Decision 310, the tribunal upheld a decision to vary conditions of registration in line with the council's policy against multi-occupancy rooms (in this instance one three bedded room).

The tribunal has also considered cases that focus on the whole ethos of a home or its specific regime. In Janet Evans v West Glamorgan Health Authority, the tribunal expanded on the qualities of fitness and added the requirement of "a caring attitude towards residents and patients and an ability to create and maintain an atmosphere free of tension amongst both staff and residents. Without such qualities as these the welfare of patients would inevitably suffer." In Hannon v Cheshire County Council (1992) Decision 192, the decision to cancel registration was confirmed in circumstances where there were concerns about client records, lack of food for residents, attitude towards staff, and fire precautions. The tribunal was concerned that, "All the indications are that the Appellant runs the home purely as a business and not as a vocation or a care centered project." The circumstances in Mattarooa v East Sussex County Council (1986) Decision 45 provide an extreme illustration. An inspector described "a regime of exaggerated repetition and strict control, with an emphasis on routine." The owner was obsessed with hygiene, including 'tongue brushing,' and insisted on daily bathing with little privacy in an over regimented fashion.

Finally, the case of Hawkins v Essex County Council (1995) Decision 291 illustrates a multiplicity of concerns pertaining in one care home for elderly residents and is worthy of brief recital. Registration was canceled due to the following: failure to employ a registered manager for over 2.5 years despite constant assurances that this was in hand and resultant inadequate management of the home; failure to ensure provision of sufficient staff adequate for the well being of residents, including employment of 16 and 17 year olds as full members of the caring staff and employing others for 72 hour weeks, and allowing an 18 year old care assistant to take responsibility for the home; failure to keep and maintain proper documentation, in particular, records of employment and an occurrence book; inadequate provision of telephone facilities for residents' use; failure to maintain fire precautions and equipment; and failure to make suitable arrangements for recording, handling, and disposing of medication. In evidence the registration officer stated, "I was shown a narrow cupboard off a corridor filled with bottles of varying quantities of liquid medicines and tablets. These had been obtained from a variety of local pharmacies and were frequently inadequately labeled. . . . Where there were labels they often did not agree with administration records . . . the quantities stocked also seemed excessive." The final concern was failure to ensure adequate recruitment, supervision, and training of staff. In finding the appellant unfit, the tribunal stated, "Mrs. Hawkins has shown a complete incapacity to manage, or be responsible for, a residential care home."

CONCLUSIONS

From just a small sample of Registered Homes Tribunal decisions included in this article, it is possible to illustrate a range of abusive practices carried on in care homes and serious levels of unfitness of some people who wish to carry on the occupation of care home managers and proprietors. The reports of tribunal decisions provide a valuable source of evidence and offer real insight into the role of inspection and developing practices. They clearly point to the need to reform this area, both in terms of process and the substance of the legislation. Current proposals for reform unfortunately relate primarily to broad issues of regulation rather than specific detail under the legislation. There is no discussion of the fit person although clarification of the qualities encompassed in this term could significantly aid the process of regulation. In the longer term it could lead to a reduction in the number of obviously unfit care home operators and an improvement in standards of care for residents.

REFERENCES

Brammer, A. (1994). The Registered Homes Act 1984: Safeguarding the elderly? (1994). *Journal of Social Welfare and Family Law, 4*, 423-437.

Brammer, A. (1996). The Registered Homes Act 1984: Ensuring adequacy or quality? *Tizard Learning Disability Review, 1*(2), 29-33.

Buckinghamshire County Council. (1998). *Independent longcare inquiry.* Buckinghamshire County Council.

Burgner, T. (1996). *The regulation and inspection of social services.* Department of Health and Welsh Office.

Centre for Policy on Ageing. (1984). *Home life: A code of practice for residential care.*

Clough, R. (1999). Scandalous care: Interpreting public inquiry reports of scandals in residential care. *Journal of Elder Abuse & Neglect, 10*(1/2).

Counsel and Care. (1995). *Under Inspection.*

Department of Health/Social Services Inspectorate. (1989). *Homes are for living in.*

Department of Health. (1992). *Inspecting social services.*

Department of Health. (1995). *Moving forward.*

Hoyes, L. & Johnson, M. (1997). Under the same roof. *Community Care*, 8-14 May 1997.

Parrott, R., Emerson, E., Hatton, C. & Wolstenholme, J. (1997). *Future demand for residential provision for people with learning disabilities.* Hester Adrian Research Centre, University of Manchester.

Public Concern at Work. (1997). *Abuse in care: A necessary reform.*

Registered Homes Tribunal Secretariat. (1985-1998). *Decisions of Registered Homes Tribunals.* London.

Ridout, P. (1998). *Registered Homes. A legal handbook.* Bristol: Jordans.

Royal College of Nursing. (1994). *An inspector calls? The regulation of private nursing homes and hospitals.* London: RCN.

Elder Abuse
in Residential Settings in Israel–
Myth or Reality?

Ariela Lowenstein, PhD, MPA

SUMMARY. The article tries to answer the question: Is elder abuse in residential care in Israel a myth or a reality? A broad definition of abuse was used, including the 'classical' forms presented in the literature, and also violation of rights and any act that infringes on quality of life of residents. As no data exist which directly explored this issue, the analysis was based on: recent laws mandating the report of abuse, governmental surveillance data, court cases, media clippings, and data from quality of life studies. Findings reveal that abuse in its 'classical' form exists only in a limited number of small private unlicensed facilities. However, when using the broader definition, abuse is a reality in many settings, exercised mainly by nurses' aides. *[Article copies available for a fee from The Haworth Document Delivery Service: 1-800-342-9678. E-mail address: getinfo@haworthpressinc.com]*

KEYWORDS. Elder abuse, residential care, quality of life, dependence, staff attitudes

INTRODUCTION

Israel entered the 'age of aging' almost two decades ago. In 1997 the percentage of the elderly (65+) in the total population was 11%,

---

Ariela Lowenstein is Senior Lecturer and Director, Center for Research and Study of Aging, Faculty of Welfare and Health Studies, School of Social Work, Haifa University, Haifa 31905, Israel. She is also Chair, Behavioral, Social Science and Research Section, International Association of Gerontology, European Region.

[Haworth co-indexing entry note]: "Elder Abuse in Residential Settings in Israel–Myth or Reality?" Lowenstein, Ariela. Co-published simultaneously in *Journal of Elder Abuse & Neglect* (The Haworth Maltreatment & Trauma Press, an imprint of The Haworth Press, Inc.) Vol. 10, No. 1/2, 1999, pp. 133-151; and: *Elder Abuse and Neglect in Residential Settings: Different National Backgrounds and Similar Responses* (ed: Frank Glendenning, and Paul Kingston) The Haworth Press, Inc., 1999, pp. 133-151. Single or multiple copies of this article are available for a fee from The Haworth Document Delivery Service [1-800-342-9678, 9:00 a.m. - 5:00 p.m. (EST). E-mail address: getinfo@haworthpressinc.com].

133

numbering 628,000 people (Statistical Yearbook, 1997). Among the Jewish population, the percentage of elderly has tripled since the creation of the State of Israel in 1948, from close to 4% then, to more than 11% today. In the Arab sector, the percentage is still low (3.1%) due mainly to high fertility rates (Azaiza, 1996). Changes are occurring in the demographic structure of the elderly population: they are aging rapidly. The number of elderly 75 years and older increased dramatically from 26,000 in 1955 to 216,000 in 1995. In addition, the number of disabled elderly increased during this period by a factor of 2.5, from 29,000 to 73,000. This group is the most vulnerable and are heavy users of health and social services, including residential care. A difference exists, however, between the Jewish and Arab populations when comparing disability rates among the 75 years and older group. Within the elderly Arab population their percentage is 22.6% compared to only 8.7% among the Jewish aged (Factor, Be'er, & Primac, 1992). These data are consistent with findings which reveal that ethnic and racial minorities suffer poorer health status and are more likely than majority group elders to develop chronic health conditions and suffer disabilities in older ages (Wykle & Kaskel, 1994).

Despite the continuing aging process of the Israeli population, the rate of institutionalization is relatively low, 4.4% (44.3 beds per 1,000 Jewish elderly in the population) as compared to 8-11% in Holland, Sweden, and Canada. This disparity exists even though the overall rate of disabilities in activities of daily living (ADL) is very similar to that of most Western countries. This situation may be related to the existence of a strong family-oriented support system and a growing network of community and home-based services (Barnea & Habib, 1992). It should be noted, however, that historically institutional care was the first type of service within the long-term care system developed in Israel, preceding community care by some fifty years (Bergman & Lowenstein, 1988). In the Arab sector, the first big modern residential facility was built only four years ago, as elderly people are still cared for by the informal nuclear and extended family. But the Arab society is in transition from a traditional, rural, and religious society to a more modern and urban one (Al Haj, 1989; Azaiza, Lowenstein, & Brodsky, 1997). These changes impact on patterns of service utilization, both in the community and in the area of institutional placement (Weil, 1995).

Despite the growing attention to quality of life and quality of care in residential services, the increased awareness of elder abuse, and the expanding professional ability to identify abuse cases, no research is yet available on abuse in institutions in Israel. Also, on the broader issue of elder abuse by family members and informal carers in the community, very limited research has been conducted (Lowenstein, Bergman, & Schwartz, 1992; Nikrug & Ronen, 1993; Lowenstein, 1995; Lowenstein & Ron, 1996; Sharon & Zoabi, 1997). Thus, the premises of this article are twofold: first, as in most modern developed countries older people are subject to ageism and hence socially devalued which might expose them to abuse (Hazan, 1997). Second, in some residential settings the impact of the 'total institution,' combined with the notions of dependency and infantilization as a social discourse, are so strong that they may also lead to abuse (Goffman, 1961; Fontana, 1978; Booth, 1985; Kayser-Jones, 1990; Hockey & James, 1993).

The purpose of this paper is to explore the phenomenon of abuse in residential facilities in Israel, based on governmental standards and regulations, on laws mandating the report of abuse, on institutional quality of life studies, and on reported cases of abuse which were brought to court and received media coverage. The main question asked is whether abuse in the institutions is a myth or a reality?

LITERATURE REVIEW

In spite of the growing body of research on the topic of elder abuse, the term is still open to question. Most studies note the lack of any agreed definition of the problem, which has been mostly examined in the community (Johnson, 1986; Wolf & Pillemer, 1989; McCreadie, 1992; Wolf, 1996). Sellers, Polts, and Logan (1992) argue that elder mistreatment includes also self-neglect and abuse by formal carers in institutions. Key issues in this respect are whose standards do we use and whose preferences determine interventions; are there any legal sanctions or regulations to deal with the problem by formal service providers? In the United States almost every state has enacted statutes that define and mandate the reporting of elder abuse (Lee, 1986). In Israel, the *Law for the Protection of Residents*, 1966 and the *Criminal Law, Amendment No. 26–the Protection of Helpless Persons, 1989* mandate the reporting of this social problem and outlines sanctions against the abusers. The aged are included in the definition of helpless persons. Such a definition, however, strengthens the notion of the dependent elderly person, whose societal value is low.

The 1989 amendment, though, reflects more public awareness and sensitises the society and formal care providers to the issue of abuse and the need to clarify the situation with regard to reporting, both in the community and in residential facilities (Kerem, 1995). According to this legislation, the macro-legal system of social control mandates any witness to incidents of abuse to report them and 'forces' the professional community to report and intervene (Lowenstein, 1995).

The complexity of the concept of abuse or maltreatment has been discussed by several researchers (Peretti & Majecen, 1991; Penhale, 1993; Tatara, 1993). Isolation, physical and mental impairment, and dependency on carers were found to be among the major variables which expose an elderly individual to forms of abuse, especially to incidents of neglect (Kosberg, 1988; Wolf & Pillemer, 1989; Lee-Treweek, 1994; Kosberg & Garcia, 1995). Data on abuse in residential facilities, however, are scarcer than on abuse in the community (Pillemer & Moore, 1989; Meddaugh, 1993; Feehan & Bailey, 1994). As Goodridge, Johnston, and Thomson (1996) suggest, 'the dynamics of elder abuse and mistreatment occurring in institutional settings are complex and incompletely understood' (p. 50). Pillemer and Moore (1990) note that 'the first obstacle encountered in examining the issue of nursing home patient maltreatment is that of definition' (p. 8).

This paper will use a broad definition of abuse covering most aspects in the literature such as physical abuse, emotional and psychological abuse (including verbal), violation of rights, financial abuse, and neglect (Sengstock & Hwalek, 1987; Hudson, 1989; Hall, 1989). It will also include violation of care, which impacts on quality of life of residents in institutions, such as lack of autonomy, de-individuation, infantilization, or harassment (Booth, 1985; Kayser-Jones, 1990). For our purpose, quality of care is defined as any area in the elderly person's life within the institution that influences his/her quality of life, i.e., including the health (medical and nursing) care and social support services, structural variables of the facilities such as staff ratio, etc. (Fleishman & Ronen, 1986).

ELDER ABUSE WITHIN THE SYSTEM OF RESIDENTIAL CARE

In 1996, 306 long-term care institutions were operating in Israel, with 23,600 beds. Israel classifies nursing home residents according to the level of care they need: the semi-independent (independent in ADL and usually limited in homemaking capacity); the frail (partially limited in ADL and suffering from mobility difficulties); the nursing (who need help with most ADL activities, are not mobile, and are usually incontinent); and the mentally infirm. Table 1 presents the distribution of beds according to level of care.

In addition there are 9,000 residents in different sheltered housing projects. According to the Ministry of Health, the number of beds in private and public institutions does not answer existing needs, and there are nearly 2,600 people on waiting lists for placements in residential facilities, mostly those requiring the nursing and mentally infirm levels of care.

There are two major sponsors of institutions: those that are owned and operated by the private sector (for profit) with 38% of the beds and those owned and operated by non-profit bodies, public voluntary organisations or the Government, with 62% of the beds, 10% of which are operated by the governmental sector. A larger number of beds for the independent elderly (about two-thirds) are operated by the public sector while half of the nursing beds are operated by the private (for profit) system. Usually the private commercially owned institutions, which operate relatively smaller facilities, rank lower as far as the physical structure, range of services offered and manpower ratio, education and training in ageing care. In recent years, though, many

TABLE 1. Level of Care and Number of Residents

Level of Care	Number of Residents	Percent of Residents
Independent	7,800	27%
Frail	7,000	24%
Nursing Care	6,900	41%
Mentally Frail	1,900	8%

improvements have been introduced into the private system (Bergman & Lowenstein, 1988; Shperling, 1990).

In 1990 68% of the residents in institutions were 80 years and older as compared, for example, to only 21% among the general elderly population; 20%, 75-79 years and only 13% between 65 to 74 years. The percentage of the 'old-old' in institutions increased in recent years: the 80 years and above increased from 58% in 1983 to 68% in 1990, and the 75 years and older increased from 81% to 88%. Most of the residents are unmarried, 81% as compared to 39% in the general population. Women constitute 71% of the residents while in the community their share is only 55% among the elderly. The condition of many of the residents deteriorated since they entered the facilities, 20% of those defined as independent became frail, and close to 20% of the frail changed their status to the nursing care level (Be'er & Factor, 1993). Thus, life in an institutional setting usually increases the dependency status of residents.

The licensing and supervisory mandate for residential care is divided between two ministries. The Ministry of Labor and Social Affairs is in charge of institutions for the well-aged and the semi-frail elderly, while the Ministry of Health is responsible for the nursing and mentally infirm elderly. The policy mandating the licensing and regulation of institutions is grounded in the *Law for Supervision of Homes, 1965* and the *National Health Ordinance, 1940,* with the amendments that have followed.

The two Ministries provide standards and regulations for care that impact on elder abuse and are authorised to press charges against any facility that does not meet the required criteria. However, 'the effectiveness of surveillance in regulating standards of institutional care has been questioned' (Fleishman et al., 1994). Among the shortcomings of governmental regulatory systems the following were mentioned: lack of clarity of the institution's areas of responsibility; partial enforcement of regulations; the existence of unlicensed facilities; methods in many countries which are neither uniform nor methodical, etc. (Day & Klein, 1987). Bearing in mind all these shortcomings, a supervisory system may still play an important role in improving quality of care and thus ensuring quality of life.

Until the mid-1980s the surveillance system in Israel was based on assessment of national supervisors and teams of the relevant governmental ministries who classified the facilities into five categories–good, satisfactory, mediocre, poor, and very poor–after rating the medical and nursing care, physical structure, staff ratios, services, and residents' satisfaction. Sixty percent of the existing facilities then were of satisfactory or good quality and 40% of mediocre or poor quality.

Due to the rapid development of Israel's long-term care system, an effort has been made to raise the level of quality of care and quality of life. As a number of homes have been closed due to inability to meet standards, steps have been taken to improve supervisory methods. Thus, since the mid-1980s the JDC-Brookdale Institute of Gerontology, cooperating at first with the Services for the Aged of the Ministry of Labor and Social Affairs and later with the Division of Geriatrics of the Ministry of Health, started to test and implement a new approach for the assessment of quality of care based on the 'tracer method' (Kessner & Kalk, 1974; Fleishman et al., 1994). The tracer method distinguishes between good and poor facilities as assessed previously by surveyors. Such an approach integrates structure, process, and outcome indicators of quality of care and uses multiple sources of information. Using this method, data compiled during the early 1990s revealed differences between licensed and unlicensed institutions on specific quality indices of personal nursing care, processes of admission, participation of residents in institutional life, cleanliness and food, physical structure, and residents' rights. The unlicensed facilities were rated much lower, pointing to maltreatment of their residents. In 1991-92, for example, among those institutions that did not succeed in renewing their license because of poor quality, five were closed and lost their licenses, and 17 were working on correcting their deficiencies (Fleishman et al., 1994). Many of these institutions, caring for frail and nursing elderly, are private (for-profit) small facilities with limited untrained manpower and do not even apply for a license; thus, the supervisors have to 'detect' them. A large number of the deficiencies which were identified in such facilities point clearly to abuse and maltreatment; for example, elderly who were left with their urine all night unchanged, elderly restrained to beds or chairs for hours, and elderly who were locked in their rooms for hours as punishment (Fleishman et al., 1996).

One of the 'strongest' examples of institutional elder abuse occurred in the beginning of the 1990s. Cases of terrible physical and emotional abuse and unprecedented neglect in a small private nursing home near Tel-Aviv, caring for 15 residents, were brought to the attention of the welfare officer-in-charge. According to the laws which mandate protection of residents and reporting of abuse, each welfare office in every local municipality has to appoint a special welfare officer (a qualified and trained senior social worker) to enforce the laws. The welfare officer was approached by some families and started to investigate the case. The report she presented to the court was very serious. In addition, the case received wide media and television coverage. The facility, which had been unlicensed, was closed and its director was sentenced to 4 years imprisonment (Kerem, 1995).

The 'tracer method' was fully implemented in 1993, as a governmental regulatory system. During 1993-1994 the method was used to locate and screen unlicensed institutions. Close to 70% of the 97 non-licensed facilities became part of the governmental licensing process. Evaluation of the surveillance system clearly proved that a direct link exists between licensing and quality of care (Fleishman, 1997).

In 1997, 57 facilities were still operating without a license, even though the *Law for Supervision of Homes, 1965* and its regulations specify the conditions under which an institution might be closed and sanctions such a director to six months imprisonment if the facility does not cease its operation. Many of the unlicensed institutions, though, are not necessarily of 'poor' quality, nor do not abuse the residents in their care. Rather, they might lack some of the physical conditions that the standards require. Most of these facilities, which are usually smaller private homes, provide care to nursing or Alzheimer patients within a 'home like' atmosphere and might lack resources to enlarge the facility. Within this list of 57 institutions, however, there are some who abuse and maltreat the residents, and a court has ordered them closed.

Despite the regulations, the governmental Ministries cannot always enforce the court orders because of the paucity of needed manpower-trained professional supervisors; the inability of the Ministries' legal units (which are usually smaller units) to act quickly; and the lack of needed alternative beds or budgetary constraints that prevent finding the appropriate solutions to residents in the above facilities (Fleishman, 1997). However, the Ministries regularly publish in the leading newspapers lists of the unlicensed homes, warning families from placing their relatives there.

In July 1997, a series of articles appeared in the media presenting the intolerable conditions in some of the above homes, pointing to extreme cases of physical, medical, and nursing neglect; lack of trained professional staff; minimal services; and serious evidence of abuse, including the use of restraints for the very sick and nursing cases. Also, refusal to provide necessary medical treatment causing the transfer of a number of elderly in serious conditions to acute hospitals (Saar, 1997). Again, the Ministries issued a warning to the public, but still the homes were not closed.

The situation outlined above was reflected in the annual report of the State Controllers' Office (1996) that asked the Ministries to be firmer and act to close unlicensed homes, enforcing the regulations and court orders (Saar, 1997). However, the lack of manpower within the supervisory system resulted in only two cases being brought to court in 1996, where orders to close these facilities were issued. The courts deliberated the case of these two private homes for two years before providing the warrants because the owners and directors of the homes did not cooperate. Moreover, some of the families discussed in court their distress and inability to pay larger sums for their relatives in other homes. Although the court issued a closing order, it gave one facility the option of operating until 1999 so it could change its conditions and improve services and become licensed. This is unprecedented, as usually the courts will allow between three to six months to obtain a license. In 1997 no cases were brought to court, even though the regional supervisors recommended it. Such cases of abuse presented above are extreme. However, one of the problems in Israel is that an ombudsman program to advocate for the rights of the institutionalised elderly has not yet been created (Fleishman, 1997).

If the issue of abuse in residential care is considered in a broader perspective to include violation of rights, which impacts on quality of life and quality of care, then some form of abuse may be found in many facilities. For example, in a focus group with directors of both public and private facilities from around the country, each has admitted that some of their staff treat residents with disrespect to the point of infantilization. Such behaviours are evident when addressing residents as 'granny,' 'sweety,' using 'baby talk,' as well as threatening them and ignoring their personal wishes for privacy and autonomy. This situation is more common among nurses' aides, as has been shown in previous studies (Fisk, 1984; Goodridge, Johnston, & Thomson, 1996).

In a study on independent residents in one home near Tel-Aviv, nurses' aides perceived their work as degrading and looked for every possible 'way out.' They viewed the residents as 'not being persons any more' or 'they are unoperating human machines' (Hazan, 1997, p. 11). Such notions reflect both ageism and the perception of the elderly as dependent unfit persons that might lead to maltreatment and abuse.

Regarding residents' rights in Israeli institutions, data show that most of the basic rights like the right for self-determination, the right for information, the right for privacy, etc., are mandated by law in the *Regulations for Supervision of Homes (maintenance of independent and frail elderly, 1986, article 36).* However, for the nursing and mentally infirm aged, such rights are not included in any legislation or regulations, reflecting again societal attitudes towards the more sick and dependent (Yacovitz, 1989). In the United States, for example, there is a legal binding code regarding the rights of this population, who are the most dependent and vulnerable (Edwards & Vildgen, 1981). Such a situation is also related to maltreatment and abuse, especially against the more dependent elderly in nursing homes, which operate on the basis of the 'medical model' that encourages dependence and depersonalisation (Bowker, 1982; Lowenstein & Yacovitz, 1995). Thus, many of the residents and their families are unaware of their rights and/or afraid to complain. This is congruent with data presented by Monk et al. (1984) who found that over half of the nursing home residents in their study had refrained from pressing any charges or complaints.

In recent years, however, more attention has been paid to issues of quality of life in residential care. During the last five years The Association for Planning and Development of Services for the Aged in Israel (ESHEL) placed high priority on improving the quality of institutional care. To achieve this goal two main approaches were undertaken. The first expanded training programs to include most of the staff in residential settings. On a national basis, training of directors of old age and nursing homes began in the mid-1980s, when ESHEL cooperated with the School of Social Work at the University of Haifa to develop a two-year certificate program. In addition, after the creation of ESHEL's Training Centre five years ago, and in cooperation with the Ministries, different professionals and para-professionals working in institutions received a variety of courses and inservice training. Also, a special one year course for welfare officers was developed (Kerem, 1991/92).

The second course of action involved the introduction of various demonstration projects. Among them a 'Quality of Life and Personal Space' project, which was an action research endeavor, based on the limited data on determinants of quality of life in institutions (Cohn & Sugar, 1991). The goal was to introduce professional and organisational changes into facilities, using a combined quantitative and qualitative approach. The research component was based on the models of person-environment fit (Lawton, 1977; Timco & Moos, 1989) using parts of the Glass (1990) quality of life model. Physical and environmental quality dimensions included scales based on the Moos Sheltered Care Environment Scales (SECS) (Lemke & Moos, 1987). The dependent variables were morale and social well-being.

The study was conducted in three non-profit medium sized (200 and 100 beds) facilities in Haifa, which include all levels of care. In each home a 30% sample of residents (N = 120) and 40 staff members were interviewed. Nearly 85% of the residents interviewed were independent and semi-frail. The average age was 83.2 years, the majority (80%) were widowed women, and, on the average, they had been living in the institutions for 3.5 years.

Table 2 presents the results of a regression analysis, using social well-being as the criteria for quality of life. The data in Table 2 reveal that most of the variance in social well-being were predicted by relations with staff and privacy-autonomy. The more privacy residents had and the more staff respected their privacy, the higher they rated their social well-being. Regarding interactions and attitudes of staff, the more respectful and warm the relations with staff were perceived to be, the higher the social well-being of residents.

Examples of resident-staff interactions from the qualitative data were: 'We really know what's good for you, and we only want to do what's good for you, so you must eat, you must have something . . . ' actually coercing the resident to have her meal by forcing food into her–in other words, abusing her. The content of the observations in this area, however, show that in two of the facilities more tension than a warm and encouraging atmosphere existed between staff and residents. In the third facility, the situation was different and staff encouraged residents to take more responsibility and have more control. In this facility residents responded much more positively on the social well-being scale than in the other two institutions (Lowenstein &

TABLE 2. The Criterion: Social Well-Being Multiple Regression Results

Predictor Variables	b	beta	F
Food and Meals	.274	.108*	4.039
Privacy	.183	.209**	4.617
Relations with Staff	.853	.398***	12.985
Physical Comfort	.320	105*	3.624
Resident Participation	.845	.082	0.248
Total F = 12.926	R^2 = .692		

*p <.05
**p < .01
***p < .001

Brick, 1995). The findings corroborate the importance of the conceptual areas of analysis included in the Glass model (1990).

DISCUSSION

Since no 'hard' data exist on elder abuse in institutional settings in Israel, it is not possible to determine how much abuse occurs, a situation that is consistent with the experience in other countries (Pillemer & Bachman-Prehn, 1991; Payne & Cikovic, 1995). Using a narrow definition that includes the 'classical' incidents of physical, emotional abuse and neglect, the data presented here demonstrate that elder abuse in residential care in Israel exists in only a limited number of unlicensed small, private facilities. In this respect elder abuse in institutions is a myth. However, if we view elder abuse as improper quality of life which includes violation of rights, lack of autonomy and privacy, infantilization of residents, and other aspects of the 'total institution,' then the phenomenon is much more wide spread.

Previous research has demonstrated that in residential settings barriers to successful implementation of the normalisation principle are often attitudes and values of the service providers (Pillemer & Moore, 1990). As presented by Clark and Bowling (1990) and other studies (Pavelich, 1994) client-staff interaction seems important in contributing to the quality of life of the individual resident. Stereotypic attitudes and inappropriate behaviour of staff, especially nursing aides, might lead to maltreatment and infringe on quality of life. This has been found in the study of personal space (Lowenstein & Brick, 1995) and in the study by Hazan (1997). Apparently, it is a more universal phenomenon that can also be related to the negative perceptions of the aged in society, to the notion of dependency, and to the work environment of residential facilities (Pillemer & Moore, 1990; Chappel & Novak, 1992; Hockey & James, 1993; Mercer, Heacock, & Beck, 1993; Goodridge, Johnston, & Thomson, 1996).

Most of the 'traditional' forms of abuse occurred in facilities caring for dependent nursing residents, mostly advanced in age, unmarried women with serious medical, behavioural, and cognitive problems. The most common types of abuse were neglect in medical and nursing care and physical and psychological abuse. Many of the personnel accused of abuse were nurses' aides, corroborating data from other studies (Fontana, 1978; Pillemer & Bachman-Prehn, 1991; Payne & Cikovic, 1995; Goodridge, Johnston, & Thomson, 1996). However, nurses' aides are the largest group of personnel in nursing home care and they, more then others, are exposed to stressful work situations and to interpersonal conflicts and violence (Pillemer & Moore, 1990). Moreover, a large body of nurses' aides in Israel have very limited training, many of them new immigrants from the former Soviet Union with language difficulties in communicating with residents also.

The more 'classical' forms of abuse happened in small private unlicensed nursing homes, whose number grew in the 1990s, as a result of the ageing of the Israeli population and the increasing rates of disability among the aged. These homes are subject to more rigid surveillance, but the appropriate ministries do not always succeed in closing them. However, using broader definitions of abuse and maltreatment, and especially infringement of basic rights and violation of quality of life, abuse has been found to be much more wide spread.

Regarding societal reaction to the phenomenon, the data indicate that it was expressed in the following five areas: First, growing public awareness was reflected by wide media coverage when serious acts were committed. Second, a changing social policy was expressed through new legislation and regulations, mandating reporting of abuse and imposing sanctions against perpetrators; the appointment of special welfare officers to enforce it; and the changing governmental surveillance system, which caused many of the unlicensed facilities to become licensed by changing their standards or to face charges. Third, the courts brought some cases to trial, and homes were ordered to be closed; in one instance, also, sentencing the director to 4 1/2 years imprisonment as noted earlier. This process, however, is still slow, a finding which is consistent with previous research (Walker, 1989; Pollack, 1995). One of the explanations is the fact that the laws and regulations in this area are relatively new. Fourth, a larger investment has been made in educational and training programs for all levels of residential care personnel and in welfare officers in charge of implementing the relevant laws and regulations (Kerem, 1991/2; Ron & Lowenstein, 1996). Increasing professionalization through education and training has proven to be a preventive measure against abuse (Pavelich, 1994). Fifth, a greater emphasis exists on raising standards of quality of care and quality of life in residential facilities through action demonstration research projects (Bergman, 1997; Lowenstein & Brick, 1995).

CONCLUSIONS AND RECOMMENDATIONS

This paper has explored the existence of abuse in institutional facilities in Israel. The data and analysis were based on governmental surveillance laws and regulations of residential settings, on laws mandating the reporting of abuse, on some court cases, media clippings, and the limited quality of life studies. Thus, the conclusions can only be partial. Within the inherent limitations of these data, the findings are still useful for considering several implications for practice, training, and future research.

By using a narrow definition of abuse we can conclude that the phenomenon of abuse in residential care is more of a myth than a reality. When we analyse and discuss it from a broader perspective, abuse is a reality. Many of the facilities are still limiting residents' rights, controlling their life, especially if they are the more disabled and dependent residents. Ageism and the perception of dependency devalue the residents (Hazan, 1997). Combined with the negative aspects of the 'total institution' this may lead to maltreatment and abuse, especially by nurses' aides.

Several suggestions follow from the above analysis. First, governmental regulations and laws of reporting should be strongly enforced, allocating more professional manpower and more resources towards this end. Second, public awareness should be constantly raised through education and media programs to change images of ageing and to sensitise the public to the phenomenon of abuse. To achieve this goal, in residential settings, ombudsman councils should be created, involving the public in 'direct' supervision of homes. Third, innovative educational and training programs should be developed for every category of workers treating aged clients such as hospitals' teams and especially welfare officers and staff working within residential facilities. Such programs should include teaching the respective laws and regulations, the meaning of life in the 'total institution,' the meaning of autonomy and control, issues of patient care, etc. Some of these topics were included in guidebooks developed for interdisciplinary and para-professional staff in institutions (Lowenstein & Ron, 1995). The police and the courts should also be included in such training programs. Finally, Israel should develop a research agenda on elder abuse and abuse in residential care, studying it from diverse perspectives; for example, estimating incidence and causes of abuse, creating profiles of the perpetrators and the victims, developing innovative intervention models, and evaluating their effectiveness.

The existence of such a phenomenon, even if it is limited, touches the very soul of the Jewish heritage of 'thou shalt honour thy mother and thy father.'

REFERENCES

Al-Haj, M. (1989). Social research on family lifestyles among Arabs in Israel. *Journal of Comparative Family Studies*, 20(2), 175-195.

Azaiza, F. (1996). Family planning among rural Moslem women in Israel. *Journal of Comparative Family Studies*, 27(3), 559-568.

Azaiza, F., Lowenstein, A. & Brodsky, J. (1997, submitted). The new phenomenon of institutionalization among elderly Arabs in Israel.

Barnea, T. & Habib, J. (Eds.) (1992). *Aging in Israel in the 1990s*. Jerusalem: Bialik (Hebrew).

Be'er, S. & Factor, H. (1993). *Census of long-term care institutions & sheltered housing program-1990*. Jerusalem: JDC-Brookdale Institute (Hebrew).

Bergman, S. & Lowenstein, A. (1988). Care of the aging in Israel: Social service delivery. *Journal of Gerontological Social Work*, 12(1/2), 97-108.

Booth, T. (1985). *Home truths. Old people's homes and the outcome of care*. Aldershot, Hants, Gower.

Bowker, L.H. (1982). *Humanizing institutions for the aged*. New York: Lexington Books.

Chappell, N. & Novak, M. (1992). The role of support in alleviating stress among nursing assistants. *The Gerontologist*, 32(3), 351-359.

Clark, P. & Bowling, A. (1990). Quality of everyday life in long stay institutions for the elderly: An observational study of long stay hospital and nursing home care. *Social Science & Medicine*, 30, 1201-1217.

Cohn, J. & Sugar, J. A. (1991). Determinants of quality of life in institutions: Perceptions of frail older residents, staff, and families. In J.E. Birren, J.E. Lubben, J.C. Rowe & D.E. Deutchman (Eds.), *The concept and measurement of quality of life in the frail elderly* (pp. 28-48). San Diego, CA: Academic Press.

Day, P. & Klein, R. (1987). Quality of institutional care for the elderly: Policy issues and options. *British Medical Journal*, 294, 384-387.

Edwards, K.A. & Wildgen, J.S. (1981). Providing nursing home residents' rights. In G.T. Hannah, W.P. Cristian & H.B. Clard (Eds.), *Preservation of Client Rights* (pp. 319-344). New York: The Free Press.

Factor, H., Be'er, S. & Primack, H. (1992). Demographic predictions, disability predictions and prediction of needs of elderly for services till the year 2000. In T. Barnea & J. Habib (Eds.), *Aging in Israel in the 1990s* (pp. 15-90). Jerusalem: ESHEL and Brookdale Institute (Hebrew).

Feehan, K.P. & Bailey, T.M. (1994). Patient and staff abuse: Rights, expectations, options and policies. *Health Law in Canada*, 43, 73-87.

Fisk, V.R. (1984). When nurses' aides care. *Journal of Gerontological Nursing*, 10, 119-127.

Fleishman, R. & Ronen, R. (1986). *Quality of care and maltreatment in the institutions for the elderly.* Paper prepared for the International Workshop on Stress, Conflict and Abuse in the Aging Family, August 25-7, Jerusalem.

Fleishman, R., Mizrachi, G., Dynia, A., Walk, D., Shirazi, V. & Shapira, A. (1994). Improving regulation of care. *International Journal for Quality in Health Care*, 6(1), 61-71.

Fleishman, R., Holzer, I., Walk, D., Mandelston, J., Mizrahi, G., Bar-Giora, M. & Yuz, F. (1996). Institutions for the elderly operating without a licence: Quality of care & the surveillance process. *Social Security*, 48, 117-128.

Fleishman, R. (1997). Regulation, assessment, follow-up and continuous improvement of care–The RAF method. *Gerontology*, 77, 55-73. (Hebrew).

Fontana, A. (1978). Ripping off the elderly: Inside the nursing home. In J.M. Johnson & J.D. Douglas (Eds.), *Crime at the top: Deviance in business and the professions.* Philadelphia: Lippincott.

Glass, A.P. (1991). Nursing home quality: A framework for analysis. *Journal of Applied Gerontology*, 10(1), 5-12.

Goffman, I. (1961). *Asylums: Essays on the social situation of mental patients and other inmates.* New York: Anchor Books.

Goodridge, D.M., Johnston, P. & Thomson, M. (1996). Conflict and aggression as stressors in the work environment of nursing assistants: Implications for institutional elder abuse. *Journal of Elder Abuse & Neglect*, 8(1), 49-67.

Hall, P.A. (1989). Elder maltreatment item's subgroup and types: Policy and practice implications. *International Journal of Aging and Human Development*, 28(3), 191-205.

Hazan, H. (1997). Another place: Old age homes as a site of modernity. *Gerontology*, 77, 8-18 (Hebrew).

Hockey, J. & James, A. (1993). *Growing up and growing old. Ageing and dependency in the life course.* London: Sage Publications.

Hudson, M. (1989). Analysis of the concepts of elder mistreatment: Abuse and neglect. *Journal of Elder Abuse & Neglect*, 1(1), 5-27.

Johnson, T. (1986). Critical issues in the definition of elder mistreatment. In K.A. Pillemer & R.S. Wolf (Eds.), *Elder abuse: Conflict in the family* (pp. 167-193). Dover, MA: Auburn House.

Kayser-Jones, J.S. (1990). *Old, alone and neglected: Care of the aged in Scotland and the United States.* Berkeley, CA: University of California Press.

Kerem, B.Z. (1991-92). Abuse of the helpless elderly. *Newsletter of the Israeli Gerontological Association*, 82 (Hebrew).

Kerem, B.Z (1995). *Social work and legal intervention on behalf of the vulnerable elderly–A guidebook.* Jerusalem: Bialik (Hebrew).

Kessner, D. & Kalk, C. (1974). *A strategy for evaluating health services.* Washington, DC: National Academy of Sciences.

Kosberg, J.I. (1988). Preventing elder abuse: Identification of high risk factors prior to placement decisions. *The Gerontologist*, 28(1), 43-50.

Kosberg, J.I. & Garcia, J.L. (1995). Common and unique themes on elder abuse from a world-wide perspective. *Journal of Elder Abuse & Neglect*, 6(3/4), 183-197.

Lee, D. (1986). Mandatory reporting of elder abuse: A cheap but ineffective solution to the problem. *Fordham Urban Law Journal*, 14, 723-771.

Lee-Treweek, G. (1994). Bedroom abuse: The hidden work in a nursing home. *Generations Review*, 4(1), 2-4.

Lawton, M.P. (1977). Impact of the environment on aging and behavior. In J.E. Birren & K.W. Schaie (Eds.), *Handbook of the Psychology of Aging* (pp. 291-305). New York: Van Nostrand Reinhold Co.

Lemke, S. & Moos, R.H. (1987). Measuring the social climate of congregate residences for older people: Sheltered care environment scale. *Psychology and Aging*, 2(1), 20-27.

Lowenstein, A., Bergman, S. & Schwartz, V. (1992). *Elder abuse in a forming society.* Paper presented at the Annual Symposium of the European Behavioral, Social Science and Research Section of the International Association of Gerontology–European Region, Bratislava, Slovakia.

Lowenstein, A. & Ron, P. (1995). *A guidebook for interdisciplinary staff in residential facilities in Israel.* Jerusalem: ESHEL and the Center for Research and Study of Aging, the University of Haifa: (Hebrew).

Lowenstein, A. & Brick, Y. (1995). The complementarity of quantitative and qualitative methods in the evaluation of institutional environments. *Aging: Clinical and Experimental Research*, 7(3), 1-3.

Lowenstein, A. (1995). Elder abuse in a forming society: Israel. *Journal of Elder Abuse & Neglect*, 6(3/4), 81-100.

Lowenstein, A. & Yacovitz, E. (1995). *The elderly, the family and the residential setting-issues and modes of interventions.* Tel-Aviv–Ramot: (Hebrew).

Lowenstein, A. & Ron, P. (1996). *Elder maltreatment by family carers in Israel:*

Typology of the victim, the abuser and etiology of abuse. A research report to the National Insurance Institute. Haifa: The Center for Research and Study of Aging (Hebrew).

Lowenstein, A. & Ron, P. (1997). In service training for professionals and para-professionals in residential facilities. *Gerontology,* 78, 73-81 (Hebrew).

McCreadie, C. (1992). *Elder abuse: An exploratory study.* London: ACIOG, Kings College London.

Meddaugh, D. (1993). Covert elder abuse in nursing homes. *Journal of Elder Abuse & Neglect,* 5(3), 21-37.

Mercer, S.O., Heacock, P. & Beck, C. (1993). Nurse's aides in nursing homes: Perceptions of training, workloads, racism & abuse issues. *Journal of Gerontological Social Work,* 21(1/2), 95-113.

Monk, A., Kaye, L.W. & Litwin, H. (1984). *Resolving grievances in the nursing home: A study of the ombudsman program.* New York: Columbia University Press.

Neikrug, S.M. & Ronen, M. (1993). Elder abuse in Israel. *Journal of Elder Abuse & Neglect,* 5(3), 1-19.

Pavelich, M.D. (1994). A violation of boundaries. *Leadership,* 2, 13-16.

Payne, B.K., & Cikovic, R. (1995). An empirical examination of the characteristics, consequences and causes of elder abuse in nursing homes. *Journal of Elder Abuse & Neglect,* 7(4), 61-72.

Penhale, B. (1993). The abuse of elderly people: Considerations for practice. *The British Journal of Social Work,* 23, 95-112.

Peretti, P.O. & Majecen, K.G. (1991). Emotional abuse among the elderly: Affecting behavior variables. *Social Behavior and Personality,* 19(4), 255-261.

Pillemer, K.A. & Moore, D. (1990). Highlights from a study of abuse of patients in nursing homes. *Journal of Elder Abuse & Neglect,* 2, 5-29.

Pillemer, K.A. & Bachman-Prehn, R. (1991). Helping and hurting: Predictors of maltreatment of patients in nursing homes. *Research on Aging,* 13, 74-95.

Pollack, D. (1995). Elder abuse and neglect cases reviewed by appellate courts. *Journal of Family Violence,* 10(4), 413-424.

Saar, R. (1997). Article series on elder abuse. *Haretz* (July) (Hebrew).

Sellers, C.S., Folts, W.E. & Logan, K.M. (1992). Elder mistreatment: A multidimensional problem. *Journal of Elder Abuse & Neglect,* 4(4), 5-21.

Sengstock, M.C. & Hwalek, M.A. (1987). *Services for elderly victims of abuse: An analysis of four model programs.* Paper presented to the Gerontological Society of America, Washington, D.C., November 1987.

Sharon, N. & Zoabi, S. (1997). Elder abuse in a land of tradition: The case of Israel's Arabs. *Journal of Elder Abuse & Neglect,* 8(4), 43-58.

Shperling, Y. (1990). The private institutional system for the chronic old age patients in Israel. *Gerontology,* 49-50, 51-78. (Hebrew).

Statistical Yearbook of Israel (1997). Jerusalem: Central Bureau of Statistics (Hebrew).

Tatara, T. (1993). Understanding the nature and scope of domestic elder abuse with the use of state aggregate data: Summaries of the key findings of a national survey of state APS & aging agencies. *Journal of Elder Abuse & Neglect,* 5(4), 35-57.

Timco, C. & Moos, R.H. (1989). Choice, control and adaptation among elderly residents of sheltered care settings. *Journal of Applied Social Psychology*, 19(8), 636-642.

Walker, S. (1989). *Sense and nonsense about crime.* Pacific Grove, CA: Wadsworth.

Weil, H. (1995). *The implementation of the Long-term Care Insurance Law in the Arab sector.* Jerusalem: The National Insurance Institute, Survey 126 (Hebrew).

Wolf, R.S. & Pillemer, K.A. (1989). *Helping elderly victims: The reality of elder abuse.* New York: Columbia University Press.

Wolf, R.S. (1996). Elder abuse and family violence: Testimony presented before the U.S. Senate Special Committee on Aging. *Journal of Elder Abuse & Neglect*, 8, 81-96.

Wykle, M. & Kaskel, B. (1994). Increasing the longevity of minority persons through improved health status. In J. S. Jackson, J. Albright, T.P. Miles, M.R. Miranda, C. Nunez, E.P. Stanford, B.W.K. Yee, D.L. Yee & G. Yeo (Eds.), *Minority elders: Five goals toward building a public policy base* (2nd ed.; pp. 22-31). Washington, DC: The Gerontological Society of America.

Yacovitz, E. (1989). Residents rights in old age homes. *Gerontology*, 43-44, 34-44.

Dealing with Institutional Abuse in a Multicultural South African Society

Gerna Conradie, RN, RMidw, RCHN

SUMMARY. The climate of socio-political transformation in South Africa together with a society of complex multicultural diversities creates enormous challenges regarding the care of the elderly in institutions. Institutional abuse in South Africa may present in a unique way, as a result of issues relating to policy and legislation and care delivery systems. The need for previously segregated groups to integrate and understand the various cultural practices of people from different socio-economic backgrounds further compounds the opportunity for abuse in homes for the aged which are undergoing transformation. *[Article copies available for a fee from The Haworth Document Delivery Service: 1-800-342-9678. E-mail address: getinfo@haworthpressinc.com]*

KEYWORDS. Institutional abuse, transformation, racial groups, cultural diversity, inequity, empowerment

INTRODUCTION

South Africa has a special situation since the various race groups in the country were separated by law for 48 years. During this period the

Gerna Conradie is affiliated with Booth Memorial Hospital, 32 Princestreet, Oranjezicht, Cape Town, 8001, South Africa.

The author wishes to thank Dr. Monica Ferreria, Director, and Ms. Karen Charlton, Chief of Research, Centre for Gerontology, University of Cape Town, for their editorial assistance and guidance.

[Haworth co-indexing entry note]: "Dealing with Institutional Abuse in a Multicultural South African Society." Conradie, Gerna. Co-published simultaneously in *Journal of Elder Abuse & Neglect* (The Haworth Maltreatment & Trauma Press, an imprint of The Haworth Press, Inc.) Vol. 10, No. 1/2, 1999, pp. 153-163; and: *Elder Abuse and Neglect in Residential Settings: Different National Backgrounds and Similar Responses* (ed: Frank Glendenning, and Paul Kingston) The Haworth Press, Inc., 1999, pp. 153-163. Single or multiple copies of this article are available for a fee from The Haworth Document Delivery Service [1-800-342-9678, 9:00 a.m. - 5:00 p.m. (EST). E-mail address: getinfo@haworthpressinc.com].

country was governed by a tricameral Parliamentary system, each chamber having its own separate government departments for the affairs of the separate population groups. The Asian group was governed by the House of Delegates and the Coloured (mixed race) by the House of Representatives. Blacks had no vote or representation at all and were governed by the House of Assembly, which was elected by white voters only. The powers of the Asian or Coloured Chambers were determined by the House of Assembly, which also governed the enfranchised white population. South Africa's first democratic elections, held in April 1994, have resulted in a representative government of national unity. The new government is committed to redress the inequalities in the social and economic fabric of society.

There are 53,000 people in homes for the aged in South Africa, which constitutes about 4.5% of the aged 65 years and older. The pre-1994 Government implemented a policy of inequitable allocation of resources that resulted in a system of care for the elderly favouring the white population. New government dispensation aims to reduce this figure to 1.5% over the next five years; state subsidies are being drastically reduced, and stricter criteria for entrance into old-age homes are being applied. Subsidies are extended only to the care of frail elderly people, regardless of the social circumstances of older adults who are less physically dependent.

Although welfare policy has changed to enable access to homes for the aged to all racial groups, these institutions are still utilized almost exclusively by white and some 'coloureds.' When they are used by other racial groups, older persons prefer homes that are for a specific cultural group. The abolition of apartheid and its resulting inequalities took place too recently to have had any real effect on addressing the discrepancies between the need for institutional care and the provision of such care for less advantaged elderly people. According to the Department of Welfare, there are at present 709 homes for white aged, 43 homes for coloured aged, four homes for Asian aged, and 40 homes for black aged in the entire country. Since there are very few academic references to elder abuse and neglect in South Africa, the author has prepared this paper on the basis of her own professional nursing experience.

It is clear from the ethnic composition of the older population, which comprises 65% blacks, 26% whites, 8% coloureds, and 2% Asian, that residential care will need to be extended to meet the needs of the majority of this age group. However, it is known that the Black and Asian population groups have to date not utilized institutional care for the elderly nor have they expressed a need for such care. In both groups, traditional custom and religious tenets prescribe not only respect for older people, but also demand that elders be cared for within the home and community. The coloured population group, especially those belonging to the lower and middle income groups, as well as all those belonging to the Muslim faith, uphold the same belief in the responsibility of the extended family. However, coloureds in the higher income group and white South Africans have been using institutional care for their elderly since the end of World War II, possibly as a result of urbanization and destabilization of the family unit.

While institutional abuse is not a new phenomenon in South Africa, there is a growing awareness that this form of malpractice is increasing. To date, little information is available in South Africa. There is an absence of references on the prevalence of abuse in institutions and much of the information is anecdotal due to a lack of research on the issue. The unwillingness of institutions and organizations to disclose incidents contributes to the lack of information.

Institutional abuse may be inflicted by individual staff members or be the result of collective staff policy interpretation. The South African Aged Persons Act of 1967 does not protect the elderly against abusive ill-treatment, and disparities between penalties for elder abuse and child abuse are enormous. In South Africa, common-law neglect of the elderly is not regarded as a mandatory punishable offence.

CONTRIBUTORY FACTORS TO ABUSE IN RESIDENTIAL CARE HOMES

Abuse of the elderly may take place in any institution throughout the world. However, in the South African context, this type of abuse presents in a unique way. To understand the context, it is necessary to consider policies and legislation, as well as cultural diversity and care delivery systems in the country.

Policy

The new government has made a commitment to take responsibility for the care of frail elderly people and/or destitute citizens of all races.

Previously, 44% of the national budget for Social Security was spent on the provision of a non-contributory means-tested old age pension and services for the elderly. But priorities in the country at present require a shift towards the re-allocation of resources for children and the provision of basic needs, such as water and sanitation, housing, education, and health care for the previously disadvantaged majority at the expense of services for elderly people.

In South Africa there are two types of institutions for the care of older people. Several non-governmental organisations own and manage homes for the aged that are fairly large institutions governed by management boards. The services of professional staff, such as nurses and social workers, are subsidized by the government, and the salaries are determined by the Department of Welfare and the Department of Health. A second group comprises institutions that are privately owned and managed. These institutions are usually smaller, and staff salaries which are determined by the owner are not subsidized. Remuneration for the staff often tends to be inadequate and non-market related, which apart from anything else may be considered as exploitation of carers.

Current Legislation

The Aged Persons Act of 1967 does not allow for the reporting of incidents of abuse of elderly persons. As a result of numerous reports and allegations appearing in the media, institutional abuse in South Africa was highlighted by a 'think tank' held in Cape Town during October 1992 that was attended by concerned professionals from organisations involved in the care of the elderly. A pressure group, the Concerned Friends for the Frail Aged (CFFA) was established subsequently in 1992 and has been active in mobilizing support to curbing abuse, especially in residential settings.

Such groups as CFFA and the South African Council for the Aged have successfully lobbied welfare ministers, and national and provincial senior welfare officials, resulting in the drawing up of strategies and guidelines for the protection of old people. For example, the White Paper of the National Department of Welfare provides a framework for care of the elderly that addresses the needs and well-being of older persons. The Guidelines for Provincial Policy on Age Management and the International Federation on Ageing's declaration on the Rights and Responsibilities of the Aged have been adopted by government. Although new proposed legislation has been tabled in Parliament by the National Department of Welfare, the White Paper has yet to be adopted at a national level. All other legislation under the New South African dispensation has only been accepted by the Legislator of the Western Cape. The other eight South African provinces have yet to follow suit and their structures for the prevention of abuse are not yet in place.

Cultural Diversity

A lack of understanding of the cultural practices and traditions between the previously segregated groups in South Africa may contribute to resentment between a carer and an older resident or between two residents from different socio-economic backgrounds. The rural black population may be considered to be community-oriented where all endeavours are directed at the communal good, and the needs of tribe, clan, or family remain a priority before those of the individual. In the white population, on the other hand, the realization of personal ambition is often considered to be more important than the needs of the group. Differences also exist in the interpretation of such concepts as privacy, personal property rights, or personal responsibility that may further lead to friction, distrust, and malicious intent between persons of different races. In some urban areas these cultural differences may be less marked. However, in a system where racism was enforced by law for a period of 48 years, it is evident that racial prejudice may not be eradicated for some time to come.

In a multi-cultural society, carers need to become aware of the influence of the cultural influences under which they operate and which affect the interaction with both colleagues and elderly residents from other ethnic groups. Unless carers are willing to move from a primarily unicultural viewpoint to one of respect and appreciation for cultural diversity, caring systems will of necessity break down.

A deterioration in the physical and mental capacity of many frail residents in old-age homes will provide a challenge to care-givers. In addition, personality changes in the older resident such as outspokenness, obstinacy, cantankerousness, and insistence on personal status may further exacerbate already tenuous relationships.

Active abuse, as manifested in incidents of physical assault and emotional abuse, occurs just as it does all over the world. Other types of abuse include the situation where a black carer may supplement or substitute prescribed medication with traditional medicine or 'muti.' This may be done particularly to contain or modify difficult behaviour in a resident. Verbal abuse also may be inflicted in any one of the eleven indigenous languages not understood by the resident.

The most commonly experienced type of abuse is financial abuse or exploitation of the resident. This may be inflicted by carers of all races, but it often stems from the historical discrepancy in material affluence between the races. A 'tip-mentality' has developed in some caring and service situations where part of the ordinary caring duties and responsibilities of staff may only be rendered on payment of a 'tip' or remuneration in cash or kind, e.g., food, jewelry, or luxury goods. Examples of such abuse are: $1.00 for a glass of water; $4.00-$10.00 for a bath; on alleging that the management requires extra payment for dessert after a meal, $0.20-$1.00 is 'charged' by the carer; and any amount is charged for the rendering of a basic service such as dusting, watering plants, or removing waste.

Care Delivery Systems

The existence of abuse in residential institutions is the result of inadequate training of carers, poor conditions of employment, and lack of care-giver support.

Recruitment and Training of Staff. Caring for elderly people provides challenges that may be emotionally and physically exhausting, and management structures often do not take account of the demanding nature of caring for the frail and confused elderly people in particular. The care delivery system derives its services primarily from the nursing model. The bio-medical model of teaching does not adequately prepare the student nurse for caring for the elderly. Furthermore, in South Africa very long working hours are the norm in the nursing profession, and 12 hour shifts are still common. Care of the elderly resident is labour intensive, often with poor conditions of service and poor remuneration, leading to low staff morale and demotivation.

The nursing profession has its roots in a system of in-service training, where traditionally the training itself was considered to be part of the remuneration, and parity of salaries has existed in the profession since the 1970s. This practice may have resulted in the nursing profession attracting persons in more recent times from cultural groups who were limited by work restrictions in other fields of employment under the previous government.

In Government subsidized institutions, in-service training for semi-skilled carers is available. Where such training does not exist, institutions will endeavour to employ persons with some training, albeit informal training. In terms of the carer-improvement policy of the new Government, employers are encouraged to select suitable candidates for training from their existing staff, thereby improving both standards of service in the institution and building up staff capacity. Such training is offered by non-governmental organizations (NGOs) such as The Order of St. John of Jerusalem and the Red Cross Society of South Africa and some tertiary colleges. Where training facilities do not exist, carers seldom acquire the necessary caring and coping skills, and it is then that abuse may result.

Screening of Carers. Currently, there is no mechanism for screening job applicants for their suitability as carers. Care of old people is not an attractive option for job seekers as it is perceived as non-stimulating. It may therefore attract persons who are unable to find employment in other fields and so may contribute to the abuse of residents.

Unstructured Conditions of Employment. In Government-subsidized institutions where employment conditions are governed by the codes of labour unions, the possibility of misunderstanding and exploitation of workers in care homes is limited. Carers function within a structured system where job descriptions define responsibilities and opportunities for abuse are fewer because of supervision and discipline. They are able to offer better salaries to even the lowest ranks of staff. Subsidized institutions also maintain a better ratio of staff to residents, thus creating a more manageable workload.

In private institutions, however, employment codes and regulations are not routinely enforced. There are no minimum training requirements, and job descriptions and service contracts are only vaguely defined. Quality of care cannot be assessed and merit appraisals cannot be completed unless there are standards against which they can be measured. It is not possible to dismiss staff for poor work performance without adequate job specifications and by the same token it is difficult to find motivation for promotion. Some carers in private institutions become demotivated and develop a casual attitude towards the completion of duties, while the more dedicated and motivated carer may seek alternative employment. Privately owned institutions have no licencing and staff requirements, only registration as a business. Owners or managers sometimes have no relevant training and employ very few nursing professionals, very often only enough to meet the requirements of legislation governing the control and distribution of medicine and drugs. Other staff such as carers, have only in-service training. No registration of semi-skilled carers exists in South Africa.

Lack of Support for the Carer. Lack of emotional support for all ranks of carers causes staff to feel that they are operating in isolation and are being exploited by management. Some subsidized institutions have the services of social workers or human resource managers who provide motivational or psycho-social support to carers, whether they are trained or semi-skilled. The threat of affirmative action and possible unemployment, together with low salaries, an unreliable and unsafe public transport system, and the high crime rate in peri-urban townships from where the majority of carers commute daily, further impact on their coping abilities. The empowerment of carers to deal with resulting feelings of insecurity and resentment is obvious.

In view of the magnitude of the apparent problem of abuse of elderly people in South African institutions and of the limited expertise of concerned professionals in combatting this problem, the need for legislation, research, theory development, diagnostic instruments, and prevention or treatment strategies have become a matter of the greatest urgency.

LEGISLATION

In spite of wide spread denial of the problem of abuse of elderly residents in South African care homes by the management of both subsidized and private institutions, awareness of this problem has increased markedly during the past five years. Both non-governmental organisations, such as Concerned Friends of Frail Aged and the South African Council for the Aged, and government institutions such as the Human Rights Commission are now lobbying for:

- The scrapping of the outdated Aged Persons Act of 1967 and its replacement with an act that effectively addresses the problem of abuse;
- A police 'elderly protection unit';
- A 24-hour Helpline to report abuse; and

- A central register of cases of abuse of the aged (van Dokkum, 1996: 18)

Other necessary future legislation might also include:

- Provision for the punishment of criminal neglect of the elderly, along the lines of the Child Care Act;
- Statutory reporting of procedures along the lines of the existing Child Care Act;
- Creation of a durable power of attorney to eliminate financial exploitation (van Dokkum, 1996);
- Extension of the provisions of the Prevention of Family Violence Act to include parents, grandparents, and cohabiters;
- Development, implementation, and accreditation of training programmes for carers in accordance with the proposals in the Green Paper on Skills Development Strategy, for Economic and Employment Growth in South Africa, of the Department of Labour of South Africa;
- Appointment of a Law Commission to draft an Act along the lines of the Older Americans Act;
- Establishment of an Office of the Ombudsman for the elderly; and
- Transfer of curatorship proceedings from the Supreme Court to a special court, such as a Family Court (van Dokkum, 1997: 17).

EDUCATION AND TRAINING

It is desirable for education and training to include:

- Public awareness campaigns to combat racism, cultural intolerance, and violence undertaken through the media, and
- Institution of a bill of rights for residents of homes for old people that will allow residents rights and enable them to be treated with dignity and respect.

In addition:

- Management should become more involved and aware of the demands of caring for the frail and confused elderly.

- Special in-service training of all nursing staff in care homes for old people should be encouraged. A two-week training period for lay health workers before appointment should be compulsory.
- Legislation concerning the employment of lay health workers needs to be drafted, as well as standards set for the training of these workers.
- A clearly defined code of conduct for nursing staff, including lay health workers is required. A comprehensive job description for this cadre of workers should be provided.
- A support system for lay health carers should be structured in order to sustain and equip them appropriately, especially in caring for the frail elderly.
- Family members should be counselled before and on the admission of the relative to a home. It is important that they have realistic expectations of the institutional environment.
- Communities should be encouraged to become involved in the activities of homes for the aged in their area (Conradie & Charlton, 1992).

CONCLUSION

The recent Human Rights Commission has identified that 'Older persons have a right to have their human rights protected, hence *Section 9 (3)* of the new *Constitution of South Africa* guarantees equality for all regardless of race, gender, sex, *age*, disability. *As a vulnerable group, older citizens, therefore have a right to rely on the state for protection. They also have a right to protection against abuse and other forms of mistreatment*' (Kadalie, 1997: 3).

The climate of socio-political transformation in South Africa together with a society of complex multi-cultural diversities creates enormous challenges regarding the care of the elderly in institutions. Although pressure groups have been successful in increasing awareness of elderly abuse, governmental legislation needs to be implemented taking into account the aspects discussed in this paper.

REFERENCES

Conradie, G. & Charlton, K. (1992). *Malpractices and mistreatment of residents of homes for the aged.* Centre for Gerontology, University of Cape Town.

Kadalie, R. (1997). *Proposal: National project on monitoring human rights of older persons.* Cape Town.

van Dokkum, N. (1996). Protection of the elderly: A need for activism. *South African Journal of Gerontology,* 5 (1).

van Dokkum, N. (1997). A durable power of attorney for older South Africans *South African Journal of Gerontology,* 6 (1).

Index